TABLE OF CONTENTS

TASK SKILLS—The Effort Necessary to Get the Job Done

TEAM SUPPORT FROM THE ORGANIZATION

TEAM LEADER FIT

WHO THIS BOOK IS FOR

This book of need diagnostics and development tips was designed for any motivated team, team member or team leader with a need at any level in the organization. This book will also help anyone who is serving as a team facilitator or team coach.

WHO THIS BOOK WON'T HELP

Any team member or team who has not yet accepted a need or limitation or weakness or developmental opportunity will not be helped by what's in this book. If the team, team member or team leader is in denial, rationalizing, confused or being defensive about having needs, nothing in this book will help.

Teams and team members who *do* accept that they have a need but *do not* have the motivation, drive, urgency or energy to do anything about it also won't be helped by what's in this book.

SO

Teams and team members who believe they have a need and want to do something about it will find most of what they need in this book. Additionally, this book references other developmental resources.

The book contains diagnostic material to tailor a general need into an actionable and focused one. Many times a team, team member or team leader will have a vague notion of what's wrong but can't quite define it. The book contains hundreds of very specific needs to choose from.

The nearly 200 tips in this book will help any team, team member or team leader who recognizes specific needs and is motivated to do something about them. If that's you or your team, read on.

FYI for Teams

(Using the scales of the TEAM ARCHITECT® and eTEAMS™)

THRUST—A common mindset about what needs to be accomplished

- **Cluster 1: Thrust Management**—Did the team set its course early and well?
- **Cluster 2: Thrust Clarity**—Were the goals and objectives of the team clear to everyone on the team?
- **Cluster 3: Thrust Commitment**—Was every team member truly committed to the goals and objectives of the team?

TRUST—Trusting others to do what's right for the team and for each other

- **Cluster 4: Trust in Truthful Communication**—Was communication inside the team open, honest and complete?
- **Cluster 5: Trust in Actions**—Did individual team members do what they said they were going to do?
- **Cluster 6: Trust Inside the Team**—Did members of the team trust each other?

TALENT—The necessary collective skills to get the job done

- **Cluster 7: Talent Acquisition and Enhancement**—Was there sufficient talent on the team to get done what they needed to do?
- **Cluster 8: Talent Allocation/Deployment**—Were the right people assigned to the right tasks?

TEAMING SKILLS—Operating the team's business efficiently and effectively

- **Cluster 9: Resource Management**—Was the team short on resources? Did the team waste resources? Did the team spin its wheels? Did the team go outside for resources or best practices?

- **Cluster 10:** Team Learning—Did the team improve by learning from its successes and failures and the successes and failures of others?
- **Cluster 11: Decision Making**—Did the team have trouble making key decisions in a timely way? Were the decisions the team made the right ones?
- **Cluster 12: Conflict Resolution**—Was there excessive noise and unresolved conflicts that took up time and kept people from working well with one another?
- **Cluster 13: Team Atmosphere**—Was the atmosphere inside the team conducive to everyone performing at their best?
- **Cluster 14: Managing Process**—Were the processes the team used to do its work efficient and effective?

TASK SKILLS–The effort necessary to get the job done

- **Cluster 15: Focusing**—Did the team have trouble setting and following priorities?
- **Cluster 16: Assignment Flexibility**—Did team members pitch in and help others get their work done?
- **Cluster 17: Measurement**—Did the team have adequate process and outcome measures to guide its work?
- **Cluster 18: Delivering the Goods**—Did the team get the job done?

TEAM SUPPORT FROM THE ORGANIZATION—How well the leadership of the organization enables the team to perform

- **Cluster 19: Team Support from the Organization**—Did the leadership of the organization enable the team to perform?

TEAM LEADER FIT—How well matched the team leader is with the needs of the team

- **Cluster 20: Team Leader Fit**—Did the team have the right leader?

WHERE DID THESE 20 CLUSTERS COME FROM?

The 20 effectiveness clusters of *FYI for Teams* come from the TEAM ARCHITECT®, a Lominger tool that covers the available research on high-performing work teams. Available in sort cards or questionnaire form, the TEAM ARCHITECT® contains 80 behaviors important to team success. Throughout the book these behaviors are included as part of the skilled definition of each dimension. They are noted by number to enable easy reference for users. The TEAM ARCHITECT® is available in an electronic 360° feedback format known as eTEAMS™.

WHERE DID THE REMEDIES IN *FYI FOR TEAMS* COME FROM?

FYI for Teams consists of nearly 200 direct tips. Where they existed, we used research findings. A rich array of research exists on high-performing teams—what effective teams do well, what stumbling teams have trouble with, what experiences teach the effective skills, what the experiences look like, and what the key drivers are. You'll see references to the best books that we've seen on the various topics in the pages that follow.

Additionally, the three authors have been in the team development business for a combined 70 years, on both the research end and the practical end. We've heard hundreds of teams and team members describe their difficulties during meetings and team-building sessions, figured out with them what's getting in their way, and have tested ideas for fixing things with them. We know from experience and research what tips are most likely to work.

ADDITIONAL REFERENCES

This book can be used as a stand-alone assessment and development source, in conjunction with the TEAM ARCHITECT® or eTEAMS™, or in conjunction with our book of a full library of competencies and tips, *FYI For Your Improvement*™. *FYI* contains 10 tips for each of the 67 LEADERSHIP ARCHITECT® competencies, the 9 PERFORMANCE MANAGEMENT ARCHITECT® dimensions, and the 19 Career Stallers and Stoppers identified in research over the decades. More extensive developmental recommendations on the same material are contained in the CAREER ARCHITECT® Development Planner. References to the 67 competencies of the LEADERSHIP ARCHITECT® appear at the end of each chapter.

FYI FOR TEAMS CONTAINS NUMEROUS RESOURCES

Tips for the 20 team effectiveness clusters (listed in each cluster of this book).

Appendix A, containing a general or universal plan for attacking any developmental need, anything you or your team wants to get better at doing.

Appendix B, a listing of the 23 LEADERSHIP ARCHITECT® Competencies that are most associated with these 20 team clusters—the 23 key characteristics (competencies) most likely to drive overall team effectiveness.

GUIDING PRINCIPLES BEHIND THE TIPS

- **1. Brief.** Most readers, being motivated people with needs, want to get started right away. They want the low-hanging fruit. They want quick help. The tips were designed to help teams get started quickly and see results as soon as they begin executing the tips.

- **2. Things every team and team member could and would do.** There are many more complex and involved problem solving methods, for example, that are not included here. In *FYI for Teams*, we assume that the team is not very good at whatever you're reading about, and would appreciate tips that don't assume you are practiced or proficient. You just want to get started and do something.

- **3. Just the 10 key tips.** Hard as it was to hold ourselves to 10 topics per dimension, we believe the 10 most likely or 10 most common topics to deal with will do you the most good. Where the topic is quite complex, we recommended a book as well.

- **4. Quick results.** While some of our topics involve longer-term effort, most are things teams can do tomorrow and hopefully see some quick improvement.

BOOK RECOMMENDATIONS

We have included book references for each dimension. Nineteen of the 20 clusters in *FYI for Teams* has two to eight sources for further reading or listening with a complete listing in Cluster 18.

We used these selection criteria:

1. **ROI:** Is there a significant and immediate payoff for reading this book? Are there developmental suggestions busy people can implement?

2. **Organization:** Is the book well laid out? Is it easy to find what you are looking for?

3. **Ease:** Is it well written?

4. **Solid:** Is the advice more than opinion?

5. **Prolific:** Are there lots of tips and examples?

6. **Available:** Is the book available?

WHAT DOES IT MEAN WHEN YOU SAY A TEAM HAS A NEED?

When it is said that the team has a weakness, there are a number of possibilities:

1. The entire team is weak on something—like setting priorities. In that case, the whole team should work on how to set priorities.

2. Some team members are not good at setting priorities, thereby causing problems for the rest of the team. In that case, those team members would work on how to set better priorities, helped by the rest of the team members who are already good at it.

3. One member of the team is bad at setting priorities and that one person is preventing the entire team from being effective. In that case, that one person needs to work on the need, supported by the rest of the team.

4. The entire team is stumbling but the causes are many. Most members have a need or two that is contributing to the less than stellar performance. In that case, each member would have a development plan on his or her specific need.

So the use of the TEAM ARCHITECT® and *FYI for Teams* could result in a team development plan on one need, a team development plan where every member works on a need, or one or more individual development plans where members work on their own needs.

HOW TO USE THIS BOOK

There are four conditions under which some development might be called for:

1. The team or one or more team members is average in a skill that needs to be higher.

2. The team or one or more team members is weak (unskilled) in an important area.

3. The team or one or more team members is untested (maybe unskilled) in an important area.

4. The team or one or more team members overuses or overdoes a strength to the point that it is causing problems for the team.

MAKE SURE THE TEAM IS WORKING ON THE RIGHT NEED

All clusters for which we have remedy topics and tips are listed in the Table of Contents. Scan this to see if you can find the need that the team is interested in working on. When you think you have found the team's need, go to that page and check for two things: 1) Are two or more of the unskilled definitions true for the team? and 2) Is the team unlike more than two of the skilled definitions? If you answer yes to both 1 and 2, you have discovered an appropriate need. In the case of an untested need (number 3 above), the unskilled statements wouldn't really describe the team because the team has never had an occasion to try or apply the skills. The way you could think about this is that if the team had the opportunity to apply that skill, the descriptions most likely would describe how the team would do. You can think of the two definitions as: This is more what the team is today or would be if the team had to do this (the unskilled definition) and this is what the team would like to be (the skilled definition). It's a before and after snapshot.

WATCH OUT FOR PHANTOM NEEDS

Sometimes even excellent feedback can identify the wrong need. Even if everyone agrees that the team is having problems with open communications, the question is why? Maybe the real problem is just that (Cluster 4) or it could be any of the other Trust clusters, or Conflict Resolution (12) or even Focusing (15). So if none or only a few of the tips for the team's identified need seem to make sense, check other likely clusters to see if the need is more likely one of these.

WATCH OUT FOR A WEAKNESS MASKING AN OVERUSED STRENGTH

Sometimes a strength used to extreme turns into a weakness. Often if we are quite good at something, such as timely Decision Making (Cluster 11), we may get into the habit of making decisions too quickly to avoid debate and conflict. If any of the overdone definitions in the clusters fit your team, we suggest some ways to compensate for this without endangering the strengths of the team. After all, if you are quite good at timely decisions, it makes little sense to do less of this. What works is to do some different things about the overdone portions and leave the strength alone. In this case, we might recommend you pay equal attention to Conflict Resolution (Cluster 12). Some team effectiveness skills you can use to compensate for *overdone* strengths are listed immediately after the overdone definition at the beginning of each cluster. Another way to find the team's real weaknesses is to read the overused definitions of your top five strengths. Sometimes you will be able to find the team's real needs that way.

STEPS FOR MOTIVATED TEAMS AND TEAM MEMBERS WITH A NEED TO DEVELOP

1. From regular feedback or use of The TEAM ARCHITECT® cards or eTEAMS™ tool, try to determine what the need is.

2. Read the unskilled definition for the need. Which bullet points describe the need best? Look to the skilled definition. What would the team like to be able to do when it is done working on this need? This is the before and after picture.

3. Check the causes that might apply. Many developmental efforts have floundered because the plan attacked the wrong problem. Write down the team's specific need—what it looks like, what causes it, who it plays out with in what situations.

4. Read the map for the need. The map gives the lay of the land. It reviews the general case of the behavior, how it operates and why it's important. Especially important to remember are things about the competency the team

ix

didn't understand before they read the map. Those extra added learnings will make a difference in the team improvement plan.

5. Look at the general plan (Appendix A) which lists 10 ways to develop in any area and pick any of those that seem to fit. This universal plan can be used as a basic core for any plan.

6. Look at the specific tips and pick the ones that apply. Each topic is written against a specific manifestation of being unskilled at the dimension. It is unlikely that all of the topics or tips will apply to any one team or person. Think back to the causes the team checked and the "why it's important" noted from the map.

7. Look at the LEADERSHIP ARCHITECT® competencies associated with the need. Each competency has a complete development plan associated with it in *FYI For Your Improvement*™ or the CAREER ARCHITECT® Development Planner. It may be that one or more team members will need to build or modify their personal development plan(s) to improve their effectiveness in the team.

8. Look at the specific *FYI* references listed for the original *FYI For Your Improvement*™. They might also be helpful when putting together the action plan.

9. Lay out a plan and a schedule. The plan should include at least three items the team will work on immediately. The team should measure the number of times they did this or didn't do that and record these efforts so they can track improvement. Set a specific timeframe of no more than a month to try these items repeatedly; if the timeframe is longer or indefinite, the team will be less likely to do anything. Start today.

ABOUT LOMINGER LIMITED, INC.

In the course of more than a decade of collaboration on research, articles, consulting projects and course development, Michael M. Lombardo, Ph.D. and Robert W. Eichinger, Ph.D. identified a frustrating and persistent gap between what research indicated were the best practices in management and executive development and the way most systems were actually being run. In 1991, Lombardo and Eichinger founded Lominger Limited, Inc., in order to develop and publish The LEADERSHIP ARCHITECT® Suite of integrated tools, a resource that gives executives, managers, and human resource professionals the ability to put research and best practices into action.

Cara Capretta Raymond, Vice President of Business Development for Lominger Limited, Inc., has over a decade of practical experience in the insurance industry, working with leaders, teams and organizations on development. Cara has designed various strategic initiatives to build integrated competency-based solutions to support selection, assessment, feedback, training and performance management. Her most recent position included designing and implementing a succession planning system to identify and develop talent in a large Fortune 500 company. Throughout her career, Cara has given feedback to hundreds of leaders using various feedback instruments including VOICES®, BENCHMARKS® and PROFILER®.

Mike Lombardo is Director of Research and Product Creation at Lominger and Co-creator of The LEADERSHIP ARCHITECT Suite. With Bob Eichinger, Mike has authored 20 products for the suite, including *FYI For Your Improvement*™, *The Leadership Machine*, the CAREER ARCHITECT®, CHOICES ARCHITECT® and VOICES®. Formerly he was at the Center for Creative Leadership for 15 years, where he was an author of *The Lessons of Experience*, a study of executive success and derailment; BENCHMARKS®, a 360 feedback instrument; and the LOOKING GLASS® simulation. Mike has won four national awards for research on managerial and executive development.

Bob Eichinger is CEO of Lominger and Co-creator of The LEADERSHIP ARCHITECT® Suite. He has been working with managers and executives on personal development for over 40 years. He has been a one-on-one feedback giver from both inside and from outside organizations. He has also served on feedback teams within courses and off-site in various organizations and public courses. He has lectured extensively on the topic of executive and management development and has served on the Board of the Human Resource Planning Society, a professional association of people charged with the responsibility of management and executive development in their organizations. Bob has worked personally with well over 1,000 managers and executives over his career providing developmental suggestions contained in this book.

1

THRUST—A common mindset about what needs to be accomplished

Thrust Management—Did the team set its course early and well?

UNSKILLED

☐ Team does not have a purpose-setting and goal-setting process in place

☐ Team does not follow a purpose-setting process

☐ Team does not have a common purpose and clear goals

☐ Team does not handle conflict around goals well

☐ Although team members disagree on goals, individual members hold back opposing viewpoints

☐ Team members are not asked for input on team purpose and goals

☐ Team and team members are totally focused on the present

☐ Team does not adjust goals to changing demands

☐ Team does not monitor progress toward achieving goals

☐ Team may not be energized or challenged by goals

SKILLED (TEAM ARCHITECT® ITEMS WITH NUMBERS)

☐ (1) Team members put disagreements on goals up for discussion and everyone on the team has an opportunity to provide input

☐ (19) Team members look ahead; they scan the environment to see what impact it will have on the work of the team and adjust accordingly

☐ (37) The team has a process that constantly monitors the accuracy of its goals and plans

☐ (55) The team sets challenging goals

1

☐ The team has a process in place to align itself with organization-wide purpose, goals, strategies and vision

☐ There is a free exchange of views and counterviews within the team about purpose and goals

OVERUSED (TOO MUCH OF A GOOD THING)

☐ The team is so much into goal-setting that nothing much else gets done

☐ The team is too rigid about its goals

☐ The team gets into endless debate without the leader calling time and moving on

☐ The team sets goals that are too high and demotivating

☐ The team sets its goals in a vacuum, shutting out external input and context

Note on overused strengths: Strengths used too much or too singly tend to have the negative effects listed above. To decrease those negative consequences, you have two alternatives. You can scale down or use the strength less, or you can compensate for it with another skill or behavior. In practice, it is very difficult to get an individual or a team to use a strength less. Therefore, the best path is to develop compensators. Below are listed other TEAM ARCHITECT® clusters that would compensate for overusing this dimension and compensating skills from the LEADERSHIP ARCHITECT® library of 67 competencies.

COMPENSATING TEAM CLUSTERS: 12, 15, 18, 19, 20

COMPENSATING COMPETENCIES: 2, 3, 9, 42, 48, 53

SOME CAUSES OF POOR PERFORMANCE

☐ Organization in which the team exists may not have goal/objective setting processes in place

☐ Team goals and objectives may be dictated by the organization or leader without input from members

☐ Team members, leader or organization may be adverse to conflict; members just want to get along

☐ A few team members may dominate/control the team

☐ Team members may be very tactical and not very strategic

☐ Team members may not be able to shift gears rapidly enough

☐ Team goals do not include measures

☐ Team leader or organization does not monitor team accomplishments

☐ Team goals are too easy or too difficult

THE MAP

If you don't know where you are going, it is unlikely you will get there, or anywhere. Teams need to work on the basics to form into high-performing units. This includes the basics of developing purpose, goals, approach and measures. Having a common thrust makes everything else a team does easier. Team members can make better decisions guided by the common thrust. Team members can allocate resources aligned to the thrust. Team members know what to spend time on. A thrust or challenge rallies people together because people aspire to be successful. The best teams spend a lot of time exploring, shaping, and agreeing on a charter that belongs to them collectively and individually. On the flip side, if a challenge or clearly established goal doesn't exist, potential teams are unlikely to become high-performing teams.

SOME REMEDIES

☐ **1. Alignment.** In some cases a team resides in an organization that has a vision, mission, a set of strategies and measurable goals. In that case, the process is one of alignment. The steps are:

■ Get a clear understanding of the organization-wide vision, mission, strategies and goals. Invite someone from the organization who is familiar with them to come and present to the team. Encourage the team to ask lots of clarifying questions. Ask about the assumptions that were used to create the vision. Ask about the risks and unknowns. Ask about any future scenarios that may affect the vision. Ask what the organization expects from this specific team.

■ In a team meeting, ask for suggestions about what parts of the organization-wide vision, mission, strategies and goals this team can add value to and support. Whether it's increased market penetration, better cost management, opening new territories, or being the leader in customer service, most teams will find pieces and parts of the organization-wide thrust they can be part of.

■ With as much specificity as possible, have the team outline the specific subgoals and tactics that support the organization thrust.

■ Put all of the goals and tactics together into one plan to see if it works, given the resources of the team.

■ Set measures ahead of time that will help the team track its performance against those goals.

■ Present the plan back to the person or function that presented the organization thrust to see if they see the plan as aligned and on target.

■ Make any adjustments that might be necessary and execute the plan.

☐ **2. Create a team charter.** A charter (a paragraph to a few pages) provides a sense of purpose, as well as a clear definition of the team's role and expectations. The best team charters are clear enough to indicate performance expectations, but flexible enough to allow the teams to create their own purpose, goals, and approach. In sum, a charter may:

■ Clarify the expectations of the team.

■ Provide focus.

■ Provide a basis for setting goals and making decisions.

■ Help team members visualize their potential—what would it look like if we are successful?

■ Communicate the team's purpose to others.

The leader or a coach can facilitate the creation of a charter. Some facilitation tips include:

■ **Pre-work**—have team members come to the session with key components for inclusion in the charter.

■ **Group participation**—have all members brainstorm and provide input in a dedicated session.

- **Create a working charter**—start with a rough draft.

- **Review and adjust**—send the rough draft back to team members and let them make additional suggestions for improvement, once they've had a chance to digest the draft.

- **Communicate**—finalize the charter with the new input and distribute it to the appropriate parties.

☐ **3. The power of purpose.** A labor of love is always pursued with more passion and energy than just a labor. If the purpose of the team isn't meaningful enough, you may want to stop right there and rethink the purpose. Here we are looking for alignment between what the individual members of the team find to be challenging and energizing and the purpose and goals of the team. Meaningful purpose and strong performance go together. So the team goals must always support its overall purpose and be aligned with the key motivators of the individual team members; otherwise the team will be too confused to succeed. Read *The Wisdom of Teams* by Jon R. Katzenbach and Douglas K. Smith to learn more. According to the authors, you can find out if the purpose is truly meaningful by asking:

- Does it constitute a broader, deeper aspiration than just near-term goals?

- Is it a team purpose as opposed to a broader organizational purpose or just one individual's purpose (e.g., the leader's)?

- Does it contain themes that are particularly meaningful and memorable to each member and the team collectively?

- Do members feel it is important, if not exciting?

If the answers are not positive, recreate a more meaningful purpose.

☐ **4. Challenge the team.** Significant performance challenges will energize teams. The research on the value of goals as a motivator generally says that moderately stretching goals motivate the most. Low goals, goals everyone can reach comfortably do not motivate nor bring about peak performance. Goals that are too high do not motivate either.

Goals that almost no one can reasonably meet do not cause people to try harder; they cause people to not try at all. Moderately stretching goals are the best. While it's hard to put a metric around what moderate means, try to think about goals 85% can reach with peak performance—people working at their best. Somewhere around that will do the trick. A common set of demanding performance challenges that the team considers important to achieve will generally lead to both high performance and a better team.

It is important to remember that performance needs to be the driver, while becoming a team remains the means, not the end. If the organization provides the team with the goals, ensure that the goals will stretch the team to perform in ways that are bigger than what any individual could accomplish alone.

☐ **5. Set early and realistic targets.** Most teams shape their purposes in response to a demand or opportunity put in their path, often by management. Teams then need to set immediate performance targets or objectives so they can start to form around their cause. The objectives need to be attainable, but not so simple that they give members a sense of false security or premature accomplishment. Early small wins or successes can help to motivate and form the team. The team leader or a facilitator can take the team through a simple exercise by asking the following:

■ Ask—What do we need to do to fulfill our purpose? (Results may be the early team objectives or targets.)

■ Ask—(Per goal) Is this goal necessary?

■ Ask—How will we prioritize our goals? What criteria will we use?

■ Ask—Who will be responsible for (each) goal?

■ Ask—How will we measure?

Initial objectives should shift members from the comfort zone of individual contributor to that of team member with a cooperative purpose. For more help, read a book on MBOs (Managing by Objectives) or go to a course on goal-setting. *More help? See FYI For Your Improvement™, Chapter 35— Managing & Measuring Work.*

☐ **6. Involve the whole team**. Get input from team members. Everyone needs to be on board with the goals for a team to reach peak performance. One of the best ways to get people engaged is to ask for their input, especially if goals still need shaping. When forming a team, make sure the team leader and members know where each member stands on the goals or prospective goals of the team. After all, not all members may have "signed up" to be part of this team and may be apprehensive. The earlier the team leader and other members find out where all stand on the goals of the team, the more likely they will be to address and resolve any conflicts. A simple exercise of round table bantering can get this started. Have a facilitator post each team goal on a flipchart and then allow team members to spontaneously call out the first thing that comes to mind when they read each goal. The facilitator should post the responses under each goal. This may be a fun way to break the ice and to get people engaged.

☐ **7. Discuss the undiscussables.** Moving toward consensus on purpose and goals usually involves some conflict. If team members disagree on the team purpose and goals, this issue needs to be surfaced. You also need to find out why there is disagreement. Since many people shy away from direct face-to-face conflict, this may not be an easy task. Have a coach facilitate an "undiscussables" exercise. Research by Chris Argyris has shown that the more issues left unsurfaced, the less well the team will work together. Use a form that looks something like this to gather the information:

Goal	Concern/Disagreement with Goal	Suggested Remedy

The coach should distribute the form to all team members and gather the information ahead of the session to look for common themes. Then the coach can review the results with the group and facilitate a candid discussion around the disagreements and suggestions for moving forward. It will be important to get the team leader and organization engaged prior to, during, and after this exercise to ensure the results can be acted upon and implemented.

☐ **8. Team goals.** It's usually a good idea to include some team improvement goals along with the business goals. Generally they would be based upon the performance of the team's last year or reporting period. Ask everyone to contribute opinions about what the team could have done better last period. If you are using the TEAM ARCHITECT®, you can do a sort on the team's current state on the clusters and items. Pick a few that the team believes are most connected to performing next period's goals. Put a plan in place to improve in those areas.

☐ **9. The discipline of goals and measures and the reality of change.** Recent research has shown that truly legendary leaders have two opposing sounding traits. One is the discipline of executing strongly against a well-thought-out plan and the other is being adaptable and open to change. This paradox—discipline and adaptability—probably extends to legendary teams. The world is changing faster than most of us are comfortable with. Success means having a plan, sticking to it, and executing the plan efficiently and effectively. At the same time, the team needs to be on the lookout for signs of change that affect the purpose and goals of the team. You can play on this paradox two ways:

■ When you set the plan, extend the discussion to include what the team would do if things change. Do a change analysis, listing likely changes inside the team, to the organization in which the team resides, and to the world outside the organization. Do change scenario planning to pre-determine how the team would respond if anticipated change occurs.

■ You can wait until something changes. The team would need a scanning discipline to detect internal or external change. When the change is detected, assemble the team of the affected individuals, and modify and adjust the plan.

In either case, a good plan will have an element in it that lays out the process for mid-course changes.

☐ **10. Create the measures**. Once the goals are established, have the team work backward to create the measures, timelines and accountabilities for achievement. What gets measured usually gets done. Ask the team how they would determine if the goals were accomplished. This process may help them to better understand the goals if they didn't already. Focus on what really matters, and not just on what sounds impressive. Use the SMART approach to goals and objectives. Are they Specific, Measurable, Actionable, Realistic and Timely? If they aren't measurable, how can their achievement be determined? Creating the measures will help to keep team members clear on the goals and assignments, which in the long run may prevent some conflict.

Here are some sample questions for the team leader or coach to ask to get the process started:

■ Ask—What are our real objectives and goals?

■ Ask—How can we track our progress against the objectives and goals?

■ Ask—How often should we measure?

■ Ask—Who else should we involve in our measurement efforts?

■ Ask—Does some of the data for these measures exist here or elsewhere? If not, how can we access the data? If so, where do we start?

SUGGESTED READINGS

Fisher, Kimball, Steven Rayner, William Belgard, and the Belgard-Fisher-Rayner Team. *Tips for Teams–A Ready Reference for Solving Team Problems*. New York: McGraw-Hill, Inc. 1995.

Katzenbach, Jon R. and Douglas K.Smith, *The Wisdom of Teams*. New York: HarperCollins. 1993.

TRANSLATION TO THE LEADERSHIP ARCHITECT® COMPETENCY LIBRARY

In order for a team or individuals on a team to perform well in this area, these are the competencies that would most likely be in play. Aside from a team improvement plan where everybody works on the same thing, some individual team members may need to work on some of these competencies. A critical number (but not necessarily all) of team members would have to be good at:

MISSION CRITICAL:

- ☐ 2. *Dealing with* Ambiguity
- ☐ 35. Managing and Measuring Work
- ☐ 50. Priority Setting
- ☐ 53. *Drive for* Results
- ☐ 57. Standing Alone

IMPORTANT

- ☐ 5. Business Acumen
- ☐ 12. Conflict Management
- ☐ 51. Problem Solving

NICE TO HAVE

- ☐ 15. Customer Focus
- ☐ 32. Learning on the Fly
- ☐ 33. Listening Skills
- ☐ 34. Managerial Courage
- ☐ 37. Negotiating Skills
- ☐ 46. Perspective
- ☐ 52. Process Management
- ☐ 58. Strategic Agility

In addition to the ten tips listed for this cluster, there are additional tips that may apply from *FYI For Your Improvement*™. Below are the four items from the TEAM ARCHITECT® that make up this cluster. The item number appears to the left of each item. Immediately below the text of each item are competency and tip numbers from *FYI*. The competency is listed first (from 1 to 67), followed by the tip number (1 to 10). For example, 33-4 refers to competency 33 (Listening), tip number 4. The tips are generally written for individual development so some adaptation might be needed in the team context.

1. Team members put disagreements on goals up for discussion and everyone on the team has an opportunity to provide input.
   12-1,2,5; 33-3,6; 34-1,3; 42-1; 57-2,3

19. Team members look ahead; they scan the environment to see what impact it will have on the work of the team and adjust accordingly.
   2-1,5; 15-1,3,6; 32-2,4; 46-1,3,4

37. The team has a process that constantly monitors the accuracy of its goals and plans.
   35-1,2,3,4,7; 50-2; 52-3,8; 53-3; 63-3

55. The team sets challenging goals.
   5-6; 35-1,3,4; 36-2,3,10; 53-1,7; 57-1

MANAGEMENT

1

THRUST

THRUST CLARITY

THRUST—A common mindset about what needs to be accomplished

Thrust Clarity—Were the goals and objectives of the team clear to everyone on the team?

UNSKILLED

- [ ] Goals exist but team members are not well informed about them
- [ ] Team members are not clear about priorities and decisions because of unclear goals and direction
- [ ] Mission/vision/goals/strategies/tactics may be unclear
- [ ] Success measures may not be in place or may be vague; achievement may be difficult to determine; there is disagreement on what constitutes success
- [ ] Team members cannot describe the steps, route, or process needed to achieve their goals
- [ ] Actual work may be disconnected from goals; individual goals may not support those of the team
- [ ] It is not clear how the goals of this team fit into the larger picture
- [ ] Mission, vision, objectives, goals and measures are not well tied together

SKILLED (TEAM ARCHITECT® ITEMS WITH NUMBERS)

- [ ] (2) Team members understand the team's goals
- [ ] (20) Team members can clearly describe their mission and vision
- [ ] (38) Team members can clearly state their measures of success (what it will take to achieve each goal)
- [ ] (56) All team members know how the goals align with their work

□ All team members can credibly communicate the mission, objectives, goals and measures of the team to others outside the team

□ Any team member can quickly bring a new team member up-to-speed on the vision, goals and measures for the team

□ Any team member knows and can explain how the output of this team creates value for the entire organization around it

OVERUSED (TOO MUCH OF A GOOD THING)

□ The team, in an attempt to make the mission and goals crystal-clear, oversimplifies things

□ The team spends too much time being certain about goals and measures that the work doesn't all get done

□ The team locks everything it does to specific goals and measures to such an extent that it loses flexibility and adaptability

□ The team spends more time creating measures than doing the work

Note on overused strengths: Strengths used too much or too singly tend to have the negative effects listed above. To decrease those negative consequences, you have two alternatives. You can scale down or use the strength less or you can compensate for it with another skill or behavior. In practice, it is very difficult to get an individual or a team to use a strength less. Therefore, the best path is to develop compensators. Below are listed other TEAM ARCHITECT® clusters that would compensate for overusing this dimension and compensating skills from the LEADERSHIP ARCHITECT® library of 67 competencies.

COMPENSATING TEAM CLUSTERS: 1, 10, 14, 18

COMPENSATING COMPETENCIES: 2, 50, 53, 65

SOME CAUSES OF POOR PERFORMANCE

□ Entire organization lacks a clear goal-setting and/or communication process

□ Objectives, goals and measures are not expected nor supported

14

☐ Lack of communication to the team around goal-setting; goals may not be fully disclosed

☐ Lack of communication within the team around goal-setting; goals may not be fully discussed

☐ Team members may be in a matrix organization and report to multiple functions or units and therefore have competing work priorities

☐ Lack of team member participation in discussing goals

☐ Team or organization may not be goal- or results-oriented

☐ Team members may not know what it takes to get the job done

☐ Team goals may not be really measurable

THE MAP

A clean, clear template makes work easier and more enjoyable. A clean and clear template of mission and goals in enough detail makes priority setting easier, resource allocation more equitable, decision making faster and measurement of success open and understandable. Team members need to be able to articulate the goals and mission of the team and relate it specifically to their job. Performance indicators need to be known and understood. Everyone needs to be on the same page and have a common mindset.

SOME REMEDIES

☐ **1. Check for total charter clarity.** Every team should have the charter talked about in Cluster #1. The charter should be a written document recording the strategy and goals of the total organization, how this team's goals support that, the tactics and work processes the team will use to reach its goals, the specific products and services the team will deliver to its customers, the resource allocation within the team, and the measures the team will use to gauge its success. Have the team leader or a facilitator spend a few hours with the team to make sure the mission or purpose is clear to everyone. By simply flipcharting the following questions, the leader or coach can gauge and improve clarity among team members.

- Ask—Do the goals of this team support the goals of the organization?

- Ask—Can you tie the goals of this team into your job?

- Ask—When we do our job well, what difference does it make to our customer? The organization?

- Do we all agree that the measures of success specified in the charter are a fair measure of success?

- Is there anything missing?

- How can we as a team improve ourselves to accomplish the goals?

☐ **2. Publish the goals.** As simple as it may seem, you need to get the team goals from the charter down on paper so they become real. *Make them short and sweet.* Limit published goals to a reasonable number so that priorities are clear. Once written and distributed, it becomes hard to argue that you didn't know about or understand the goal(s) of the team. Post them in the workplace. Laminate a copy so everyone on the team can carry them around.

☐ **3. Drive for goal clarity and alignment.** Aside from having a charter and having a charter that is well understood by all on the team, making sure the charter is translatable into day-to-day work is key. Ford's "Quality is job one" doesn't leave much to the imagination. On the other hand, what does it mean for me on the assembly team? Can I slow down the assembly line to do it right? Can I reject a fender that I don't think reaches standard? Can I request that the team up the assembly line from me redo a job that doesn't look right? In simple terms, what are the rules of engagement? After everyone is knowledgeable about the charter at the team level, there is one additional exercise. How does it translate to what I do? Have each team member write down and present to the rest of the team what the goals mean for that person's job.

☐ **4. Drive for measurement clarity and alignment.** People love to have something to measure against. Aside from gauging personal worth, it can be motivating, leading to everyone doing his or her best. So it's very important that the measurements be clear, open and understandable by all. Have

THRUST

2

CLARITY

a session where the measurements are discussed. Have team members present how they will operate their specific job to achieve the goals. Make sure everyone agrees that this is the best way to measure success.

☐ **5. Validate and market the measures.** Since the mission of the team is generally directed by the organization, or at least is in the context of the organization's goals, it makes good political sense to feed the goals and measures back to the sponsor(s) or area(s) that chartered the team. Nothing would be more demoralizing to team members than to find out months into the year that they were working on the wrong goals and measuring the wrong indicators. Get the goals and measures firmly approved before publishing and communicating to the rest of the organization.

☐ **6. Align the products and services.** What outcomes and work need to get done to achieve the team goals and mission? How is the work product different from the organizational mission or individual objectives? How will the team know they are done? Have the team members figure this out in the early part of the year. The more they can visualize what success looks like and the deliverables they will be held accountable for, the more likely they'll develop an early understanding of what the team charter really is.

☐ **7. Sell in the goals.** It doesn't do anyone any good to write up the goals if you don't share and communicate them for external clarity and understanding. Have the team leader and team members present the goals to others in the organization who have to participate in the strategy or are impacted by the results. Team members should articulate the goals the same way. One of the best ways to learn or understand something is to have to present it to others. And, of course, be open to suggestions and criticism.

☐ **8. Make the goals and measures open and visible.** Ever notice how athletes keep their eye on the clock and the scoreboard? They're checking their progress against time, the competition and ultimately, winning the game. Use signs or technology to post team goals, data and progress toward accomplishment. Straightforward devices like the United Way thermometer or posting key numbers serve as constant reminders of progress.

☐ **9. Monitor measures and clarity constantly.** Talk about the team goals and individual accountabilities on a regular basis in team meetings or other encounters with team members. Have each individual discuss his or her work as part of the team meeting agenda. Scheduled discussion around goals helps to ensure understanding. Set some parameters around how each person presents an update.

Create a format or use something like this:

- Status on assignments from last meeting
- Status on individual objectives (ahead of target; on target; if not, why?)
- Impact of individual objectives on achieving team goals
- Individual and team targets on the horizon; new assignments
- Potential roadblocks or barriers to goals; actions to remove barriers

☐ **10. Team improvement.** Turn each success and stumble into a learning opportunity. Where lack of clarity of any element of the charter leads to less than stellar performance, make that a topic at a staff meeting. What went right? What went wrong? How could the charter have been made more clear and useful? Apply those lessons to the next period.

SUGGESTED READINGS

Barner, Robert W., *Team Troubleshooter.* Palo Alto: Davies-Black Publishing. 2000.

Fisher, Kimball, Steven Rayner, William Belgard, and the Belgard-Fisher-Rayner Team. *Tips for Teams–A Ready Reference for Solving Team Problems.* New York: McGraw-Hill, Inc. 1995.

Katzenbach, Jon R. and Douglas K. Smith, *The Wisdom of Teams.* New York: HarperCollins. 1993.

Parker, Glenn M., *Cross-Functional Teams.* San Francisco: Jossey-Bass, Inc. 1994.

TRANSLATION TO THE LEADERSHIP ARCHITECT® COMPETENCY LIBRARY

In order for a team or individuals on a team to perform well in this area, these are the competencies that would most likely be in play. Aside from a team improvement plan where everybody works on the same thing, some individual team members may need to work on some of these competencies. A critical number (but not necessarily all) of team members would have to be good at:

MISSION CRITICAL:

- ☐ 27. Informing
- ☐ 35. Managing and Measuring Work

IMPORTANT:

- ☐ 5. Business Acumen
- ☐ 15. Customer Focus
- ☐ 46. Perspective
- ☐ 65. *Managing* Vision and Purpose

NICE TO HAVE:

- ☐ 33. Listening
- ☐ 47. Planning
- ☐ 49. Presentation Skills
- ☐ 50. Priority Setting
- ☐ 52. Process Management
- ☐ 58. Strategic Agility
- ☐ 67. Written Communications

THRUST CLARITY 2

In addition to the ten tips listed for this cluster, there are additional tips that may apply from *FYI For Your Improvement™*. Below are the four items from the TEAM ARCHITECT® that make up this cluster. The item number appears to the left of each item. Immediately below the text of each item are competency and tip numbers from *FYI*. The competency is listed first (from 1 to 67), followed by the tip number (1 to 10). For example, 33-4 refers to competency 33 (Listening), tip number 4. The tips are generally written for individual development so some adaptation might be needed in the team context.

2. Team members understand team goals.

   3-6; 27-1,2,5; 33-3; 35-2,5,7; 36-3; 60-1

20. Team members can clearly describe their mission.

   5-6,10; 15-1,3; 27-1,4; 65-1,2,4,9

38. Team members can clearly state their measures of success (what it will take to achieve each goal).

   27-2,3,6; 35-1,2,5,7; 52-3,8; 65-2

56. All team members know how the goals align with their work.

   27-1,4; 35-1,2,3,4,7; 50-2; 47-1,7

3

THRUST COMMITMENT

THRUST—A common mindset about what needs to be accomplished

Thrust Commitment—Was every team member truly committed to the goals and objectives of the team?

UNSKILLED

- ☐ The goals of the team are not equally attractive to all the team members
- ☐ Team may not demonstrate passion for its mission
- ☐ Some team members are loners and not supportive of the team as a whole
- ☐ What the team needs to do is not very exciting or motivating
- ☐ Team members do not have their eye on the customer
- ☐ Team may not be aware of, nor have values that complement those of the rest of the organization
- ☐ Some team members aren't carrying their share of the load

SKILLED (TEAM ARCHITECT® ITEMS WITH NUMBERS)

- ☐ (3) There is an observable sense of commitment in the team
- ☐ (21) Team members are committed to their collective work goals and products—which can only be achieved by all pulling together
- ☐ (39) All team members feel responsible for customer commitments
- ☐ (57) Team members are expected to share the values of the organization
- ☐ The team works well together
- ☐ There is infectious enthusiasm in the team; members keep each other motivated

☐ Each team member feels like he or she owns the goals of the team

☐ The team celebrates wins together

OVERUSED (TOO MUCH OF A GOOD THING)

☐ Commitment to the charter is too much of a litmus test for approval in the team

☐ Teams works together so much that individualism is lost

☐ Team spends too much time on being a team and too little time performing

☐ People in the team help others so much that their individual goals are not met

Note on overused strengths: Strengths used too much or too singly tend to have the negative effects listed above. To decrease those negative consequences, you have two alternatives. You can scale down or use the strength less or you can compensate for it with another skill or behavior. In practice, it is very difficult to get an individual or a team to use a strength less. Therefore, the best path is to develop compensators. Below are listed other TEAM ARCHITECT® clusters that would compensate for overusing this dimension and compensating skills from the LEADERSHIP ARCHITECT® library of 67 competencies.

COMPENSATING TEAM CLUSTERS: 1, 7, 8, 15, 18

COMPENSATING COMPETENCIES: 21, 31, 36, 53

SOME CAUSES OF POOR PERFORMANCE

☐ Lack of buy-in among team members regarding purpose of team

☐ The work the team does is not inherently interesting or challenging

☐ The work the team does is all individual work; there is no reason to act like a team

☐ The work of the team is divided in such a way that only a few have the interesting and motivating work and others don't

☐ One or more members of the team are doing most of the work

THRUST 3 COMMITMENT

- ☐ Little role clarity, accountability or performance measures with consequences
- ☐ The team has one bad apple that causes noise for everyone else
- ☐ Lack of incentive or compensation aligned with team performance
- ☐ Company culture doesn't support the energy or focus of the team
- ☐ Lack of customer focus in organization or team
- ☐ There is so much turnover in the team that it's been hard to gel
- ☐ Team and/or organization hasn't identified values

THE MAP

People do their individual best when they are challenged and motivated by the work itself, personally invested in the products and services produced, and the customers served. No group ever becomes a team until it can hold itself accountable collectively as a team. High-performing teams are deeply committed to their purpose, goals and methods. The highest performing teams also have members who are committed to one another. This double commitment to the charter and to each other is the key to sustained high performance.

SOME REMEDIES

- ☐ **1. Vision the outcomes.** Walk the team through a visioning exercise. Ask them to envision the team finishing its work and reaching all of its goals successfully. Ask what it would look like. How would customers feel? What's in it for the team? How would each member of the team feel? Why was the team successful? What did it do well? What did it avoid doing? What kinds of rewards and consequences would there be? Would all of the above be motivating or satisfying for the team? To what extent would all of the above be possible because the team operated as a team and not just a collection of individuals? If this exercise does not produce excitement in the team, then you need to rethink the goals or lower your expectations.

☐ **2. Plan for small wins.** Break the journey toward the goal into small trips. Small wins are invaluable to building members' commitment and overcoming the inevitable obstacles that get in the way of achieving meaningful long-term purpose. Set up benchmarks along the way. Measure success in increments. Celebrate the small wins along the way.

☐ **3. Develop team values, norms and rules of engagement.** Walk the team through a series of exercises to determine the team values, supporting norms, and rules of engagement statements. These are generally basic attributes that have to do with respect and openness as well as guidelines around timeliness, workload and contribution to the team. These guiding values and rules help the team to create an environment of open communication and build commitment to high performance.

☐ **4. Develop an operating contract within the team.** Let the team members develop their roles and responsibilities. There is a certain amount of natural discovery that has to occur within the team to determine the strengths and weaknesses of its members. Once this happens, the team can decide how to apply its human resources to its goals. This process leads members to some heart-felt discussion around who may be best (and worst) suited for specific tasks along with how all the individual roles and assignments come together to achieve a successful outcome. Don't equate team with sameness in roles. Effective teams deploy resources based on human strengths and weaknesses, rather than trying to fit people into a cookie-cutter mold.

☐ **5. Distribute the work evenly among members.** Teams won't be successful over the long-run if only a few of the members are doing all of the work. If members perceive they are carrying equal loads, they are more likely to band together to achieve their goals.

☐ **6. Distribute the challenges evenly.** Most teams have some fun work and some less so. Try to evenly divide the challenging parts of the work among the team members. An even better goal is to match each challenge with the needs of each team member. Some are motivated by some aspects of the work and some by different tasks. It is natural in teams for the most challenging work to go to some combination of the most senior, been there the longest, or the most talented—those who would do best at it. Avoid this. Strive for balance and alignment. Involve the team in this division of labor. The members probably know best.

☐ **7. Develop a team theme.** Teams have a tendency to form around a favorite topic or theme that symbolizes its basic purpose or identity. The Kodak "Zebra Team" is a classic example of how a team utilized black-and-white logos, apparel and other symbols to communicate their charter of raising the status of black-and-white film. (Source: *The Wisdom of Teams.*) The best themes happen naturally, and many times by accident, or from a funny event that caused the team to bond or come up with something clever. Take, for instance, a reengineering team formed at a large insurance company in 1994 that was charged with redesigning the acquisition and underwriting process for life insurance. One of the team members from Mississippi announced that all of the unnecessary steps and handoffs in the underwriting process were as useful as a bunch of "dead cows lying in the middle of the road." While team members were initially caught off guard by his quirky sense of humor, they ended up rallying around their commitment to eliminate "dead cows" in the underwriting process. By the time their project ended, the underwriting process went from taking weeks—and up to 40 process steps and handoffs—to a matter of days and seven key process steps to get a new life insurance policy on the books. If a team theme or symbol doesn't arise naturally, have the team brainstorm to see whether there is a theme in the work that could be used as a rallying point.

☐ **8. Address lack of or slips in commitment by individual members of the team.** Find out what happened to cause this problem. One bad apple or less motivated team member can spoil it for the rest. If a team member is not as committed as the others, he or she will impact and frustrate the rest of the team, especially if he or she is still reaping the same benefits and rewards as the rest of the team. The team leader and team members need to confront this behavior.

Ask a few questions:

- Was this person committed before?
- If so, what has changed?
- Can the situation be reversed?
- How can the team and the leader address the problem?
- If this can't be reversed, what role should this person be playing (elsewhere)?

☐ **9. Involve the customers.** Bring customers into your organization if the team's activities have direct consequences for customers. Have team members visit the customer's site to see what happens to the goods and/or services the team supplies. Link communications, schedules, technology and any other support systems you can think of to make sure both organizations reap the maximum benefit from their partnership. Getting customers and team members to work closely together generally builds commitment on both sides and leads to a win-win link.

☐ **10. Include your customer in decisions.** Read *From the Ground Up*, by Edward E. Lawler, III. He says, "Feedback from customers is critical not only to the team's motivation but also to the team's ability to know what to do and whether it is doing its work well. As a result, how an organization defines its customer, both internally and externally, is crucial to a team's effectiveness." He goes on to say that teams should interact directly with the external customers who make buying decisions about services and products. It is especially true for **problem solving** or **consulting teams**. Although the beneficiaries of problem solving teams will most likely be their co-workers in the organization (because their mandate is usually to improve internal operations), the teams should still use external customers to gather information on what actually constitutes an improvement in the product or service.

SUGGESTED READINGS

Fisher, Kimball, Steven Rayner, William Belgard and the Belgard-Fisher-Rayner Team. *Tips for Teams: A Ready Reference for Solving Team Problems.* New York: McGraw-Hill, Inc. 1995.

Katzenbach, Jon R. and Douglas K. Smith, *The Wisdom of Teams.* New York: HarperCollins. 1993.

Lawler, Edward E. III., *From the Ground Up.* San Francisco: Jossey-Bass, Inc. 1996.

TRANSLATION TO THE LEADERSHIP ARCHITECT® COMPETENCY LIBRARY

In order for a team or individuals on a team to perform well in this area, these are the competencies that would most likely be in play. Aside from a team improvement plan where everybody works on the same thing, some individual team members may need to work on some of these competencies. A critical number (but not necessarily all) of team members would have to be good at:

MISSION CRITICAL:

- ☐ 35. Managing and Measuring Work
- ☐ 53. *Drive for* Results
- ☐ 60. *Building Effective* Teams

IMPORTANT:

- ☐ 36. Motivating Others
- ☐ 42. Peer Relations
- ☐ 43. Perseverance
- ☐ 50. Priority Setting
- ☐ 65. *Managing* Vision and Purpose

NICE TO HAVE:

☐ 15. Customer Focus

☐ 22. Ethics and Values

☐ 43. Perseverance

In addition to the ten tips listed for this cluster, there are additional tips that may apply from *FYI For Your Improvement*™. Below are the four items from the TEAM ARCHITECT® that make up this cluster. The item number appears to the left of each item. Immediately below the text of each item are competency and tip numbers from *FYI*. The competency is listed first (from 1 to 67), followed by the tip number (1 to 10). For example, 33-4 refers to competency 33 (Listening), tip number 4. The tips are generally written for individual development so some adaptation might be needed in the team context.

3. There is an observable sense of commitment in the team.

    35-1,2,3,7; 36-3; 53-7; 60-1,3,7; 110-4

21. Team members are committed to their collective work goals and products—what can only be achieved by all pulling together.

    36-3; 53-1,3; 60-1,3,5,6,7; 65-2; 110-4

39. All team members feel responsible for customer commitments.

    15-1,2,3,4,8,9; 35-2,7; 50-3; 53-3

57. Team members are expected to share the values of the team and the organization.

    22-1,2,3,4; 60-1,5,6,7,8; 51-8

4

TRUST—Trusting others to do what's right for the team and for each other

---

Trust in Truthful Communication—Was communication inside the team open, honest and complete?

UNSKILLED

- ☐ Team members aren't willing to stand alone and voice critical thoughts, ideas and feelings
- ☐ Team avoids internal conflict
- ☐ Issues are not out in the open; undiscussables exist and may be brewing beneath the surface
- ☐ Team may not take the time to identify, understand or leverage individual differences, including both strengths and weaknesses
- ☐ Team members may not be forthcoming or honest with one another
- ☐ Team members are stuck in their ways of doing things
- ☐ Issues are discussed but they are discussed off-line; not so much in public or out in the open
- ☐ There are cliques in the team that keep information from others
- ☐ Team is arrogant and not willing to examine itself critically
- ☐ Some team members are not truthful communicators

SKILLED (TEAM ARCHITECT® ITEMS WITH NUMBERS)

- ☐ (4) Team members speak up and say what's on their minds
- ☐ (22) Team members take the time to understand one another's differences and expertise
- ☐ (40) Team members are open with one another about their viewpoints

COMMUNICATION

4

TRUST IN TRUTHFUL

29

4

☐ (58) Team members are receptive to candidly observing and improving their own team process

☐ Issues are always surfaced in public and solved collectively

☐ Team members help each other to surface issues sensitively

☐ Team members give others time to vent

☐ Team goes into problem solving mode when issues are surfaced rather than finding blame or dismissing

OVERUSED (TOO MUCH OF A GOOD THING)

☐ Team spends too much time collecting input from members

☐ Members are overly critical of one another and themselves

☐ There is too much raw negative information being surfaced

☐ Team spends too much time focusing on the negative

☐ Team meetings end up with members getting too personal

☐ Team spends too much time reengineering their processes

Note on overused strengths: Strengths used too much or too singly tend to have the negative effects listed above. To decrease those negative consequences, you have two alternatives. You can scale down or use the strength less or you can compensate for it with another skill or behavior. In practice, it is very difficult to get an individual or a team to use a strength less. Therefore, the best path is to develop compensators. Below are listed other TEAM ARCHITECT® clusters that would compensate for overusing this dimension and compensating skills from the LEADERSHIP ARCHITECT® library of 67 competencies.

COMPENSATING TEAM CLUSTERS: 9, 11, 12, 15, 18

COMPENSATING COMPETENCIES: 10, 12, 23, 36, 51, 60

SOME CAUSES OF POOR PERFORMANCE

☐ Members are adverse to conflict

☐ Team may be afraid to take risks

☐ Organizational culture may be "too nice"; cultural boundaries stifle open communication

☐ Members lack courage

- ☐ Team dismisses differences and diversity
- ☐ Members don't trust one another; trust has been betrayed
- ☐ Members get their feelings hurt or experience too many misunderstandings with direct communication
- ☐ Members fear rejection or failure if they speak up
- ☐ Members may be non-learners
- ☐ Members may be shy
- ☐ There is little interest in making this a team
- ☐ There are cliques that keep to themselves
- ☐ Team is new and has not yet formed
- ☐ There is one bad apple that spoils it for the rest
- ☐ Team has some bad history that is still having an effect

THE MAP

False information, hidden agendas, lack of openness, late information and interpersonal noise all chill team performance. Successful teams have an open, timely and truthful communication process. Members on successful teams understand one another. They spend as much time listening and understanding as they do speaking. Members on high-performing teams take risks, trust others and resolve conflict. This requires teams to practice frank and open communication. This can be a challenge if the organization doesn't view this type of communication as "politically correct." To be successful, the team has to make it safe to openly communicate with a lot of give-and-take.

SOME REMEDIES

- ☐ **1. Honesty is the only policy.** Trust is often slow and hard to develop and easy to lose. The first step in gaining trust is to ensure that it is deserved. Have members of the team commit to being honest about what's on their minds. Some cornerstones of building trust are admitting mistakes, keeping confidences, following up on commitments, not softening the message to avoid conflict or discomfort, and promptly revealing critical information. New teams start with low levels of trust. People are testing each other and norms of acceptable behavior are forming. Team members can encourage open communication and trust by:

■ Being dependable—someone on whom the team can rely to deliver on commitments

■ Pitching in and helping other team members who need assistance

■ Reading and responding to non-verbal cues that suggest a lack of openness

■ Candidly sharing views and encouraging others to do the same

More help? See FYI For Your Improvement™, Chapter 29—Integrity and Trust.

☐ **2. Make it safe.** Team members should not play games with each another. If they don't know, they should just say so. If they aren't sure, they should ask for input. Straightforwardness builds an expectation that people will be constructive with one another. Withholding information, ideas or feelings can be destructive in teams. Some members, of course, don't have the courage or the tools to be forthright and candid when they communicate. Therefore, norms need to be established where straight talk can prevail. Environments where people are regularly asked for their input, are listened to and accepted for their differences in opinions, make it safe to speak up. Team members need to be succinct and factual, avoid inflammatory language, and perhaps most dangerous of all, avoid making sweeping generalizations, to make team members more comfortable with speaking up. So be candid, but keep it local and specific. *More help? See FYI For Your Improvement™, Chapter 34—Managerial Courage.*

☐ **3. Respect the opinions of others.** The best teams are made up of people with the biggest diversity of perceptions, who first learn to understand and value the opinions and views of others. Read *The New Why Teams Don't Work— What Goes Wrong and How to Make it Right* by Harvey Robbins and Michael Finley. They say, "Trust without respect is like a sandwich without bread." They indicate that if you don't or can't respect someone, especially on your team, you

32

will never trust them. People generally don't openly give respect to others; rather, they are stingy with it and think it needs to be earned. If you are stingy with respect here are some things you can do:

- Acknowledge that it is at least partially your problem. Everyone deserves a basic level of respect.

- Focus on the task, not the person.

- Avoid gossip—it kills respect. Form your opinions about your teammates from your workings with them, not from the second-hand gossip you may hear from others.

☐ **4. Leverage differences.** Use a coach to administer a tool (FIRO-B, Myers-Briggs Type Indicator (MBTI), etc.) on personality style, type or team roles. Have the coach use some of the common exercises with such tools to help members understand each member's preferences, how they can best contribute to the team and what their liabilities might look like. Typical exercises include what is comfortable and difficult for each type (style) to do, what each style can gain from the other, and simulated problem solving situations where each type can see what valuable perspectives another brings to the problem. Identify ways to incorporate this newly discovered information into team roles, assignments and responsibilities. Find ways to leverage strengths and create developmental opportunities for individuals while at the same time minimizing situations where people may not be temperamentally suited for tasks or assignments. Use this process to balance the team. Remember, thinking the same often occurs when a team has been together as a unit for more than three years according to some research. So use all the naturally occurring diversity of views you can. It prevents staleness. One caution: don't confuse personality with effectiveness, which is a common misuse of the above-mentioned tools. *More help? See FYI For Your Improvement™, Chapter 14—Creativity.*

☐ **5. Value diversity.** More diverse teams outperform narrow teams in problem solving tasks, especially where the task has some uniqueness to it. People do not need to be the same or think the same to work well together and be a successful team. Rather, successful teams utilize the differences to achieve the team's common purpose. Following are tips to

33

help teams value diversity:

- Remember that reasonable people can and do differ with each other.
- Try to learn as much as you can from others.
- Evaluate a new idea based on its merits (not who submitted it).
- Avoid comments and remarks that draw negative attention to a person's unique characteristics.
- Don't ignore differences among team members.

If you or someone on the team needs to work on a diversity related issue, *see FYI For Your Improvement™, Chapter 21— Managing Diversity.*

☐ **6. Exchange information.** Create a regular process or meeting time for the team that is focused on information sharing. Use some guidelines or agenda norms that make it commonplace for each member to come prepared to discuss their status on assignments, things they've learned from internal or external customers, organizational issues that may impact the team's performance, etc. Encourage all members to ask questions and to challenge one another on issues. Information sharing can help team members to develop a greater appreciation of one another based on their communication, technical abilities and performance, rather than personalities or style preferences. The team leader sets the stage for open communication. The leader's behavior is crucial in building trust and opening communication. The leader must encourage discussion of problems and key issues and then model a response that is non-judgmental. First, it must be seen as OK to ask for help or to seek the advice of other team members. Second, the leader should support (and feel comfortable with) the concept of subgroups of team members working together. This letting go is critical for group growth.

☐ **7. Face-to-face is the best space.** The correct layout of the physical space in which teams operate can be critical to success. Open communication can be best facilitated when people work in close quarters and have an opportunity to get to know and observe each other on a regular basis. Sometimes you just have to keep people talking to each other until they finally feel comfortable. Throw them in the same room and force them to hammer out working relations. One expert says that self-managing work teams seem to require both interaction time and common physical space—members may be spread out over a large facility, but they definitely need dedicated meeting and gathering spaces to allow them to operate as a team. Common space and high levels of personal interaction are also critical for most **project teams** because their members come from different backgrounds and are usually only together for a short period of time. As a result, they need activities that cause them to talk to each other.

☐ **8. Debrief successes and failures.** A regular debriefing process can help to facilitate both open communication and learning. The process can also elicit both good and bad feedback about the team, their work processes and individual contributions. This type of group debrief might help to create an environment that makes it more comfortable for team members to give and take feedback. Have a coach or facilitator ask and flipchart answers to the following questions after a key accomplishment or setback:

- What went well?
- What should we have done differently?
- What did we learn?
- How can we apply that learning?

Before jumping into the exercise establish ground rules to be used during the discussion, i.e., all comments will be presented as constructively as possible, or members will share all thoughts and not withhold feelings, etc. Also, make sure each member contributes at least one response to each of the questions. Use the learnings for future challenges or situations that might be similar so as to not make the same mistakes twice.

☐ **9. Cross-functional communication challenges.**
Glenn M. Parker, the author of *Cross Functional Teams*, found the following factors that led to poor communication among cross-functional teams:

- Lack of appreciation for the other functions

- Turf battles
- Different jargon
- Different work orientations
- Different degrees of interest in the team's outcome
- Mistaken goals

Establishing a set of operating norms will help to overcome these challenges (and not excuse them). Members of **cross-functional teams** are there because they have something to contribute. The concept of the cross-functional team is that the outcome will be better because it has been created by the combined expertise of people from a variety of functions. Viewing a problem or an issue from many vantage points is the strength of the cross-functional team. However, the value of divergent views can only be realized when there is a free flow of information.

☐ **10. Assign an issue manager.** When tough issues surface that are tilted more toward the personal rather than the factual, assign a member of the team to be the issue manager who is not an involved party. That person controls the agenda, speaking times, and problem solving tactics the individuals use to settle the issue. As the issue referee, that person cannot get involved in the issue. The task is to manage it through to completion. The role is essentially to treat the problem as a problem, even if it is personal. What are the causes, the viewpoints, the theories people are operating under? As in any conflict situation, the manager must get people to be specific and talk about feelings rather than just show them. *More help? See FYI For Your Improvement™, Chapter 12—Conflict Management.*

SUGGESTED READINGS

Becker, R. and F. Steele, *Workplace by Design: Mapping the High Performance Workscape.* San Francisco: Jossey-Bass, Inc. 1995.

Fisher, Kimball, Steven Rayner, William Belgard, and the Belgard-Fisher-Rayner Team. *Tips for Teams: A Ready Reference for Solving Common Team Problems.* New York: McGraw-Hill, Inc. 1995.

Katzenbach, Jon R. and Douglas K. Smith, *The Wisdom of Teams.* New York: HarperCollins. 1993.

Lawler, Edward E. III., *From the Ground Up.* San Francisco: Jossey-Bass, Inc. 1996.

Parker, Glenn M., *Team Players and Teamwork.* San Francisco: Jossey-Bass, Inc. 1990, 1996.

Parker, Glenn M., *Cross-Functional Teams.* San Francisco: Jossey-Bass, Inc. 1994.

Robbins, Harvey and Michael Finley, *The New Why Teams Don't Work—What Goes Wrong and How to Make it Right.* San Francisco: Berrett-Koehler Publishers, Inc. 2000.

TRANSLATION TO THE LEADERSHIP ARCHITECT® COMPETENCY LIBRARY

In order for a team or individuals on a team to perform well in this area, these are the competencies that would most likely be in play. Aside from a team improvement plan where everybody works on the same thing, some individual team members may need to work on some of these competencies. A critical number (but not necessarily all) of team members would have to be good at:

MISSION CRITICAL:

- ☐ 12. Conflict Management
- ☐ 33. Listening Skills
- ☐ 34. Managerial Courage
- ☐ 44. Personal Disclosure
- ☐ 57. Standing Alone

IMPORTANT:

- ☐ 29. Integrity and Trust
- ☐ 42. Peer Relationships
- ☐ 60. *Building Effective* Teams

NICE TO HAVE:

- ☐ 21. *Managing* Diversity
- ☐ 22. Ethics and Values

☐ 45. Personal Learning

☐ 56. Sizing Up people

In addition to the ten tips listed for this cluster, there are additional tips that may apply from *FYI For Your Improvement*™. Below are the four items from the TEAM ARCHITECT® that make up this cluster. The item number appears to the left of each item. Immediately below the text of each item are competency and tip numbers from *FYI*. The competency is listed first (from 1 to 67), followed by the tip number (1 to 10). For example, 33-4 refers to competency 33 (Listening), tip number 4. The tips are generally written for individual development so some adaptation might be needed in the team context.

4. Team members speak up and say what's on their minds.

    12-2,5,7; 34-1,2,3,7; 57-2,8,9

22. Team members take the time to understand one another's differences and expertise.

    21-4,5,6,9; 33-2,3; 42-6; 56-1,3; 60-5

39. Team members are open with one another about their viewpoints.

    29-1,2,4,7; 33-2,3; 34-2,3; 44-7,8

58. Team members are receptive to candidly observing and improving their own team process.

    12-1,2,5,7; 27-2; 34-2,3,4; 35-2,7

5

TRUST—Trusting others to do what's right for the team and for each other

---

Trust in Actions—Did the individual team members do what they said they were going to do?

UNSKILLED

- ☐ Members leave each other hanging and don't give support
- ☐ A few members politic for decisions they prefer off-line
- ☐ Members act two-faced and bad-mouth decisions made by others on the team
- ☐ Members contradict their own values; say one thing, do another
- ☐ Team operates in a vacuum and doesn't relate well or interact with other teams
- ☐ Team openly criticizes the work of other teams without trying to help
- ☐ Some team members agree with a decision in the meeting and then question it after the meeting
- ☐ Some team members are working their own agendas without regard for the team as a whole

SKILLED (TEAM ARCHITECT® ITEMS WITH NUMBERS)

- ☐ (5) Team members back each other up
- ☐ (23) Team members may disagree with a decision, but they will still support it
- ☐ (41) Team members "walk their talk"; stated values equal actual behavior
- ☐ (59) Team members work well with other teams and are seen as cooperative

☐ Team surfaces and resolves its issues and problems openly as a team

☐ Team members on the losing side of a decision act in line with the rest of the team, while still taking legitimate opportunities to make their point

☐ Team members keep conflicts within the team private to the team

☐ All team members operate within the rules of engagement agreed to by the whole team; they act and behave within the norms and values

OVERUSED (TOO MUCH OF A GOOD THING)

☐ Team members with opposing views give up too soon just to keep the peace

☐ Team may only select those candidates for membership who already walk and talk like the team prefers, thereby passing up some fruitful diversity

☐ Team is so cooperative and supportive that it doesn't get its own work done

☐ Team is so values and norms driven that individual members give up their urge for doing something different

Note on overused strengths: Strengths used too much or too singly tend to have the negative effects listed above. To decrease those negative consequences, you have two alternatives. You can scale down or use the strength less or you can compensate for it with another skill or behavior. In practice, it is very difficult to get an individual or a team to use a strength less. Therefore, the best path is to develop compensators. Below are listed other TEAM ARCHITECT® clusters that would compensate for overusing this dimension and compensating skills from the LEADERSHIP ARCHITECT® library of 67 competencies.

COMPENSATING TEAM CLUSTERS: 1, 7, 12

COMPENSATING COMPETENCIES: 12, 21, 31, 53

SOME CAUSES OF POOR PERFORMANCE

☐ Some individual members aren't trustworthy

- [ ] Some team members have a private agenda contrary to the team's agenda
- [ ] Some team members have poor peer relationship skills
- [ ] Some team members have poor interpersonal/social skills
- [ ] Team doesn't finish making decisions in team meeting, and team leaves things hanging
- [ ] Team and/or organization has not defined its values
- [ ] Team members are too competitive with one another
- [ ] Team members sabotage one another
- [ ] Team doesn't handle conflict about decisions well

THE MAP

One aspect of a high-performing team is the trust each member has in one another. Individual members have to feel comfortable taking tough and decisive actions under tension and conflict, knowing that the rest of the team is there to back him or her up. They need to know that if they go out on a limb on behalf of the team, that there isn't someone cutting the branch behind them. Positive team players will argue their points with intensity during team meetings and decision making processes, but, win or lose, they will support the outcome publicly as if it were their own preference. Negative team members bad-mouth the work of the team, try to revisit decisions that are already made, and do not support their teammates. They will try to politic off-line hoping to sway key members of the team without the other side being there to defend itself. Team players must speak with pride and enthusiasm about their team and the decisions that have been made, regardless of their own personal position. Just as individuals need to support all internal team goals, they also need to support the team in all interactions *outside* the team. This includes working with other teams and functions in the organization.

SOME REMEDIES

- [ ] **1. Set the example for others.** The improvement process begins with the rest modeling the best. If this is an area of concern for the team, have each member commit to being better at walking the talk of the team. Walking the talk requires a strong set of personal convictions, open communication with others, and a lot of self-awareness. Have each member of the team ask him or herself:

- **Do people know what I stand for?** If not, find ways to communicate what performance means to you. Be clear about what your values are and the team will align their expectations accordingly.

- **How do others perceive me?** If you don't know, find out. Get 360° feedback. How others perceive your actions may determine how likely they will be to support you.

- **Do I look for ways to demonstrate my convictions?** If not, find ways to make supportive comments to the team and about the team.

- **What do I do or say that may lead others to think I'm not in line with the team?**

- **What is the difference between what I do or say and what the most respected member of the team does?**

☐ **2. No off-line processing.** Nothing frustrates a team more than to spend time investigating and deliberating an issue, and reaching a decision, only to have it reopened by a few members off-line. Off-line processing betrays trust in the team. One of the key rules to high-performing teams is that members can't pull rank. It's facts and solutions that rule and they have no rank. If a team is truly all for one and one for all, decisions need to be made "in-house" and adhered to by everyone. Team norms should include consequences for off-line processing. The more you let this one slip, the less likely members will be to roll up their sleeves to put a lot of effort into the problem solving and decision making process the next time. Off-line processing and politicking by its very nature shows disregard for others. Those that rely on off-line influence to have their way are usually the weakest team members from a teamwork standpoint. *More help? See FYI For Your Improvement™, Chapter 29—Integrity and Trust.*

☐ **3. The real meaning.** When someone does not appear to be supportive of the team effort, the team has to examine why. What is it that a team member isn't supporting? Has the team considered that maybe the person has a point? Rather than just condoning a team member who is neither backing teammates nor supporting decisions that were made by the team, it is important to find out the reason he or she is not being supportive. Did the team member challenge the decision while it was being made? Was the challenge heard? Did the challenge have merit? Did the team listen? If not, why? Was it because of his or her style? Was it because the team didn't want to truly examine what the team member was saying, because it would have meant major changes in implementation? Many times a discordant team member acts out because he or she has trouble getting heard. Before the team decides the person isn't a team player, the team needs to give the person a fair forum. If, after fully heard and then collectively rejected, the person still is not supportive, then the team has a deeper issue.

☐ **4. Re-establish team norms.** If there are people causing trouble by not supporting team members or team decisions, you should consider revisiting team norms to deal with them as a group. The team leader (or team coach/facilitator) should facilitate a discussion of team member expectations at team meetings. Develop a list of norms or acceptable behaviors. These should be things like attendance at team meetings, decision making, dealing with conflict, supporting the team to outsiders, etc. Team norms have two functions: 1) They provide a guide for self-monitoring by team members, and 2) They provide a basis for the team leader or member to give feedback to a member who has violated a norm. Use the discussion on developing a set of team norms to assess how well the norms are currently being followed. The team must be open to change if something is not working. Assuming everyone is right in their hearts and wants the team to succeed, most problems center around a lack of communication and the absence of a forum for complete discussion of tough issues.

☐ **5. Give timely private feedback.** If we assume that the team has already established values, norms and the rules of engagement, giving quality feedback should be easy and expected. But the reality is that giving critical feedback isn't always easy. Rather than looking at it as confronting the person, consider that you are confronting the ineffective behavior that is causing the entire team to suffer. Do it first in private. Be specific about how the person's behavior is impacting you and/or the team. For instance, "Joe, when you mention to a senior leader that you disagree with a decision the team has made after the fact, it hurts the credibility of the team, and it causes the organization to doubt that we can continue to work together effectively." Give the person an opportunity to respond, but be sure to then agree to next steps to resolve the damage that has already been done or to ensure that it doesn't happen again.

☐ **6. Get the other boss involved.** If the team is a **project or cross-functional team** and the team member causing the trouble reports to someone other than a team member, you may want to consider getting the other boss involved. Maybe there is more to the story. Maybe he or she can provide some insight into this person's behavior and help you fix the situation. Or, the boss might be willing to take the person back so that you can replace the member with someone who better matches the values of the team.

☐ **7. Give the naysayer the boot.** If you've tried everything mentioned up to this point, you may need to consider removing the trouble-making team member from the group. Some people may just refuse to modify their behavior, even after they've been given feedback and a chance to present their side. And sometimes you can't fix the damage that has been done. If that is the case, they may need to be transferred or fired. While it's dangerous to generalize too much, many teams have had trouble with those who personalize decisions (how it affects them only), those on a mission who think their approach is the best one, those out for personal advancement, gossipers, and chronic conflict avoiders who just can't overcome an obstacle. Any of these have to change or go.

☐ **8. Identify barriers to working with other groups.** Different teams in organizations generally don't work well together. **Cross-functional teams** do not manage their boundaries well, do not get the support they need, do not get the resources they require, and fail as a result. Here are the causes for breakdown in the process identified by Glenn M. Parker, author of *Cross-Functional Teams.*

- **Stereotyping**—Preconceived ideas about how certain groups behave

- **Competition**—Teams compete for things like budget dollars, opportunities to work on high-visibility projects, etc. Some competition among teams is healthy. But if a team tries to achieve a goal at another's expense, i.e., by not sharing resources or information, it is negative competition that can stand in the way of healthy collaboration, a key to successful cross-functional teamwork.

- **Differentiation**—As groups become more differentiated in their practices, the challenge of integrating them increases. Although this differentiation helps units pull together to get the work done, it can be a barrier when they have to work collaboratively with a cross-functional team. Tension builds because the need to maintain differentiation is at odds with the need to integrate efforts.

If you think your team has barriers to working with other groups in the organization, ask the following questions:

- Are there any past problems that need to be resolved or overcome?

- Are you in competition with this group?

- Does this group stand to lose as a result of your team's project?

- Does this group support the concept of cross-functional teamwork?

- Do you respect this group?

Once the team has identified the actual barriers, it can prepare a plan for overcoming them and achieving successful relationships with stakeholders.

☐ **9. Build bridges. Cross-functional teams** also need to pay attention to relationships outside the boundaries of their team. Here are some tips to help:

- **Identify the key stakeholders**—List all the people and groups the team needs to be successful. What do you need from these stakeholders? Make another list of the people and groups who have something to gain and lose from the work of your team.

- **Look for commonalities**—Look beyond what you need from the stakeholders on your list to see what you can do for them. List the ways they need your ideas, your help, etc. This list should be a set of common objectives—outcomes you both share. Use this list to remind the team of the allegiance that could be formed.

- **Communicate**—Find ways to tell others about your team. Make presentations to stakeholders. Ensure that each team member representing a functional department is keeping his manager informed and "sold" on the team's project.

- **Assign boundary managers**—Carefully select the team members who will handle the key interfaces. Ask what needs to be done and who the best person is to do it. Don't assume it is the team leader.

- **Be credible**—The above-mentioned strategies only work if the team members are credible. Do other people trust you? Can they count on you to deliver the goods? If you want to enhance your relationships with key stakeholders don't ask for more than you need, don't promise more than you plan to deliver, don't set a due date you can't meet, and don't exaggerate project benefits or results.

☐ **10. Fester prevention**. A major problem for teams is when they let things fester, which almost always makes things worse. The reason for this is that most people do not seek out face-to-face conflict. Also, most teams have inadequate conflict resolution skills and routines. In general, the sooner you address a problem in the team, the easier it is to solve because a significant portion of most team problems is due to incomplete communication. Each team has to design and execute a method for the quick surfacing of issues of trust and supporting the team. Generally, it's the responsibility of the leader to put issues on the agenda, to model conflict resolution practices, and to support individual team members seeking resolution of trust issues. But each team member can play his or her part. The steps are:

- Confront as gently as possible the person directly to see whether this issue of trust can be solved locally. Seek the counsel of a mentor or friend on how best to address the problem. Stick to behaviors. Keep it impersonal.

- If that approach fails, then have a private discussion with the boss. Seek his or her counsel on how to proceed.

- If that fails, then you will have to surface the issue with the rest of the team in an issue surfacing process as a regular part of the team agenda.

SUGGESTED READINGS

Fisher, Kimball, Steven Rayner, William Belgard and the Belgard-Fisher-Rayner Team. *Tips for Teams—A Ready Reference for Solving Common Team Problems.* New York: McGraw-Hill, Inc. 1995.

Parker, Glenn M., *Cross-Functional Teams.* San Francisco: Jossey-Bass, Inc. 1994.

Parker, Glenn M., *Team Players and Teamwork.* San Francisco: Jossey-Bass, Inc. 1990, 1996.

TRANSLATION TO THE LEADERSHIP ARCHITECT® COMPETENCY LIBRARY

In order for a team or individuals on a team to perform well in this area, these are the competencies that would most likely be in play. Aside from a team improvement plan where everybody works on the same thing, some individual team members may need to work on some of these competencies. A critical number (but not necessarily all) of team members would have to be good at:

MISSION CRITICAL:

- ☐ 12. Conflict Management
- ☐ 22. Ethics and Values
- ☐ 33. Listening
- ☐ 42. Peer Relationships
- ☐ 44. Personal Disclosure
- ☐ 60. *Building Effective* Teams

IMPORTANT:

☐ 18. Delegation

☐ 27. Informing

☐ 57. Standing Alone

NICE TO HAVE:

☐ 29. Integrity and Trust

☐ 31. Interpersonal Skills

☐ 36. Motivating Others

☐ 37. Negotiating

☐ 40. *Dealing with* Paradox

☐ 53. *Drive for* Results

In addition to the ten tips listed for this cluster, there are additional tips that may apply from *FYI For Your Improvement*™. Below are the four items from the TEAM ARCHITECT® that make up this cluster. The item number appears to the left of each item. Immediately below the text of each item are competency and tip numbers from *FYI*. The competency is listed first (from 1 to 67), followed by the tip number (1 to 10). For example, 33-4 refers to competency 33 (Listening), tip number 4. The tips are generally written for individual development so some adaptation might be needed in the team context.

5. Team members back each other up.

42-1,2,5,6,7,9; 57-2,6; 60-1,7

23. Team members may disagree with a decision, but they will still support it.

12-1,2,3,4; 40-2,4; 53-1; 60-6; 65-4,7

40. Team members "walk their talk"; stated values equal actual behavior.

22-1,2,3,4,5; 27-1,2,9; 40-4; 44-8

59. Team members work well with other teams and are seen as cooperative.

12-1; 27-5; 31-2,3; 36-4; 37-7; 38-4,8; 42-5,6

6

TRUST—Trusting others to do what's right for the team and for each other

Trust Inside the Team—Did members of the team trust each other?

UNSKILLED

- ☐ Team members perform more like a collection of individual contributors than a team
- ☐ Team members compete with each other
- ☐ Members do and say things to get ahead at the expense of others
- ☐ Team may not spend adequate time together to gel
- ☐ Individuals are focused on getting their own results and don't look out for or help others
- ☐ Team lets some individual members fail or slip behind
- ☐ There is little interest in improving as a team
- ☐ Team members are following their own agenda without much regard for the team agenda
- ☐ There is distrust inside the team

SKILLED (TEAM ARCHITECT® ITEMS WITH NUMBERS)

- ☐ (6) Team members sacrifice their own needs for the good of the team
- ☐ (24) Little or no internal competition undermines team efforts
- ☐ (42) Team members put effort into building team cohesion
- ☐ (60) When one person struggles, other team members are there to help
- ☐ The team acts as one
- ☐ Team members motivate one another

49

☐ The team defends itself against unreasonable criticism from outside

☐ The team spends scheduled time improving itself

☐ Helpful feedback regularly occurs

OVERUSED (TOO MUCH OF A GOOD THING)

☐ Team spends too much time focused on internal morale at the expense of performance

☐ Too much collaboration makes the team lose momentum

☐ Members may help each other out but neglect their individual priorities

☐ Individual strengths may get lost due to the emphasis on the team

☐ Individuals may hesitate to go against the learnings of the team for fear of causing internal conflict

☐ Team may support laggard members too long and be hesitant to address performance problems in a timely way

Note on overused strengths: Strengths used too much or too singly tend to have the negative effects listed above. To decrease those negative consequences, you have two alternatives. You can scale down or use the strength less or you can compensate for it with another skill or behavior. In practice, it is very difficult to get an individual or a team to use a strength less. Therefore, the best path is to develop compensators. Below are listed other TEAM ARCHITECT® clusters that would compensate for overusing this dimension and compensating skills from the LEADERSHIP ARCHITECT® library of 67 competencies.

COMPENSATING TEAM CLUSTERS: 7, 8, 9, 12, 15, 18

COMPENSATING COMPETENCIES: 13, 35, 50, 53

SOME CAUSES OF POOR PERFORMANCE

☐ Some team members may be selfish

☐ Some team members may be overachievers and highly competitive

☐ Members may have poor peer relationship skills

☐ Team is too focused on the technical or business issues at the expense of the people issues

☐ Team may not spend enough time together to build trust

☐ Some team members may be poor fits; weak team member links

☐ Reward systems may not be aligned to support teamwork over individual performance

☐ Team has some history of trust issues that is hard to patch up

☐ Team may have poor conflict resolution skills

THE MAP

Collections of individual performers are more plentiful than well functioning teams. You might think it is reasonable to expect people to get along and work smoothly together. However, the reality is that teamwork usually takes the backseat to uneven individual performance. Most people, regardless of level or role in an organization, possess skills that are most closely linked to the strengths of individual contributors. In fact, most people never develop greatly beyond that profile. Individual responsibility and self-preservation remain the rule; shared responsibility based on trusting others is the exception. The majority of reward and incentive systems are targeted at individual performance. teaming skills are more rare than performing skills. Team leaders are more rare than leaders of a collection of individuals. High-performing teams develop after members collaborate to overcome obstacles that get in the way of team success. When teams overcome barriers and challenges, the members build trust and confidence in one another's abilities. They also reinforce each other's intentions to pursue the team purpose above and beyond individual or functional agendas. The payoff is that high-performing teams outperform the collective results of a collection of individual performers.

SOME REMEDIES

☐ **1. Formal team building.** Bring in a team coach to help the team with its forming process. Don't do just the feel good, warm and fuzzy light stuff. Go to an Outward Bound facility and take some risks as a team. Learn to understand each other in an unrelated environment outside of work. Create a situation where everyone's skills get discovered and where no one has an advantage because of rank, tenure or technical expertise. Arrange for team members to leave their comfort zones and depend on one another. Use exercises where individual performance means nothing if the team's performance doesn't prevail. (Many exercises are impossible to complete unless everyone contributes.) Make sure the exercises focus on team outcomes, not individual success. Also, make sure the outcomes can be translated into meaning back on the team.

☐ **2. Align reward systems.** What is the incentive for team members to make sacrifices? Will they be recognized or rewarded for doing so? Has the performance management and compensation system been aligned to measure and reward team performance? If not, why? If people are put on a team, but evaluated by their supervisors and compensated for individual work, it is unlikely that the team will reach optimal performance. This is especially so if raises are distributed from a competitive or rank order rating system. Follow the cash because money talks. There has to be a consequence for not being a good team member. Similarly, there should be a reward for the group doing it well. Work with your compensation department to align a performance management tool where team members can evaluate each other's performance and be compensated for the team's results. What seems to work best is a combination of individual and team rewards and incentives. The balance depends upon the extent to which working as a team produces superior results. The more that this is true, the higher the proportion of rewards need to be for team effort.

☐ **3. Develop the performance capability of others.**
What happens if a member on the team is struggling with performance? Does it frustrate other team members? How do they respond? Do they complain about that person to the other team members? Do they go to the boss? Do they shun that person because of it? If other team members recognize the performance gap and see the path to recovery, why aren't they helping that person discover it? Do they want the other member to fail? Team members should take the lead in bringing the person along. Developing others takes time

more than anything. And since developing others is generally the worst rated competency across studies, use this as an opportunity to improve someone's performance and grow a skill that most don't have. *More help? See FYI For Your Improvement™, Chapter 19—Developing Others.*

☐ **4. Spread the credit around.** One way to build trust is to be generous with acknowledging other people's accomplishments. Some of the most valuable team members with the best ideas are also the same members who can single-handedly destroy trust on the team. Do some members insist on taking all the credit or attention for work? If so, learning to shine the spotlight on others in the team can help. If members are genuine with their recognition of teammate accomplishments, trust will grow. Can individuals on the team be sincere? Do they share? Most of us are pretty selfish, so giving credit does not come naturally. Work on a system of proportional credit to spotlight the contributions of all contributors. Most of the time, many contribute to an outcome even though one person might be the main contributor. Work with the dominant contributors on the team and help them thank others who helped. Who copied the report at the last minute before the meeting? Remember that stealing someone's thunder is one of the worst things a teammate can do to betray trust on the team. Read *The New Why Teams Don't Work—What Goes Wrong and How to Make it Right* by Harvey Robbins & Michael Finley. They have an entire chapter dedicated to team trust.

☐ **5. Look for lack of trust danger signals.** Know what the signs are of trust breaking down in the team. Are people talking about one another behind their back? Are members withholding information and resources? Are they undermining one another to benefit themselves? Are they stifling their feelings? Are they blaming or criticizing one another? Do members feel like they need to cover their tracks? Is there off-line processing going on? Are there cliques? Any of these behaviors can crash the trust in a team. Confront the warning signs and talk about the issues right away. Bring in a coach or facilitator if things get too heated. Revisit the team's values to look for violations of the rules of engagement and identify the positive behaviors that can get the team back on track. Trust takes a long time to build and a short time to break down. And remember that the majority of trust issues are due to incomplete and inadequate communication. Then, human nature being what it is, we begin to wonder if the work is distributed fairly, if others are really committed, and so on. *More help? See FYI For Your Improvement™, Chapter 29— Integrity and Trust.*

☐ **6. Help a sinking team member.** Most teams don't get to select their teammates directly. Sometimes we don't know what we've got on the team until it is too late. Everybody has problems, but some have bigger problems than others. Working in close quarters will allow team members to develop a lot of insight regarding on and off work situations. Members might discover that a teammate's performance problems are linked to some other outside issue. Is the team member late all the time? Tired? Disoriented? Some of these symptoms may be linked to physical or emotional problems. Some might be a result of a domestic problem (impending divorce or trouble on the home front). And some may be caused by alcohol or drug abuse. If a problem is suspected, don't speculate or gossip. After all, if you had the problem, would you want to be judged or helped? Get the team leader involved and let the leader work with professionals to help the member. It might be as simple as giving the person feedback. Most companies have policies in place to deal with drug or alcohol abuse. And, most companies have EAP programs to help with other non-work issues. The important thing is to seek to understand first, and then provide the help or support the team member needs to get back on track.

☐ **7. The cross-functional contradiction.** We know that most functions, departments, units and businesses don't generally work well with each other. So when we group people together that represent different functions on a **cross-functional team**, we can expect some conflict and holding back. In fact, anticipate regular bumps in the road. Working on a team that has a specific purpose, while at the same time reporting to a functional boss can create some conflicts of interest. It's like working in a matrix organization where you are pulled between two different bosses and you don't know how to set priorities. The team must feel like each member makes the team a priority so that it can build trust. Members can't feel like others are merely attending meetings to spy on the various functions that are represented. Members need to take ownership for the information they exchange between the team and their function (and vice versa) and do it in a manner that is resourceful for both sides. Since trust takes time, there should be a couple of meetings where the team just gets to know one another and sets its charter and rules of engagement before tackling the task.

☐ **8. Help new team members get onboard.** New team members and leaders are added all the time to already formed teams. Teams can't get too comfortable with the way things used to be once there is a new member. This may cause some sacrifice and temporarily slow down the performance of the team. However, the team needs to roll their sleeves back up and spend some time re-forming. Otherwise, the new team member won't get a fair start and will most likely struggle adapting into the new environment. The team should create an orientation process for the new member. Here are some ideas of things to include to help ensure the success of the new member:

- Team charter and goals. Check for clarity to make sure the new team member understands the purpose of the group. Given the fresh perspective, does the member have any value-adding suggestions?

- Role clarity for the new member. Map out his or her role and explain the roles of other members.

- A candid assessment of how the team is doing. What's working, what isn't, what's needed.

- Team supplier, customer, and competitor data.

- Team values and rules of engagement. It is a good idea to revisit and perhaps amend the values to include the new team member's. You can't just expect him or her to have the same values initially.

- Organizational boundaries and guidelines the team follows. Political or cultural issues.

- Miscellaneous group processes (regular meeting times, presentations, workflow, etc.).

- Skills or competencies needed for success on the team
- Training to learn needed technical or functional skills

Finally, assign the new team member to a buddy who will be responsible for ensuring that the orientation is executed. Make this person accountable for the new team member's on-boarding process. Rather than holding back until the rest of the team is sure the person is the right fit, assume fit and let events prove otherwise. Trust first.

☐ **9. Vision team success.** Have the team imagine working together much better than they are now. Have someone flipchart the answers to the question: If we worked better together, we would be able to do what? What outcomes would be possible? What do we have to do individually and collectively to bring that off? What rewards would there be at the end of the team rainbow? Nothing breeds a success culture like winning. Great generals and coaches have always known this and make extensive use of symbols of success and small wins:

- Team dress, team parties, team celebrations, and secret team language are all signs of a tight-knit unit that believes in itself.

- Great coaches often overprepare for the lesser teams. Great generals often take the easy cities first. They do this to build a culture of success, near invincibility and to discourage opponents. What are five quick small wins your team can have that are visible, tied to your goals, and have the smell of success? Success, not rah-rah, builds confidence.

☐ **10. Team learning.** Have each member of the team read and report back on one book about leadership listed in this book. Have each member find and study a successful team in fact or fiction, current or in the past, and report back on why that team did particularly well. Desert Storm? Putting out the oil fires in Kuwait? The Los Angeles Lakers? Put the team in the role of being team experts.

SUGGESTED READINGS

Barner, Robert W., *Team Troubleshooter.* Palo Alto: Davies-Black Publishing. 2000.

Fisher, Kimball, Steven Rayner, William Belgard and the Belgard-Fisher-Rayner Team. *Tips for Teams—A Ready Reference for Solving Common Team Problems.* New York: McGraw-Hill, Inc. 1995.

Katzenbach, Jon R. and Douglas K. Smith, *The Wisdom of Teams.* New York: HarperCollins. 1993.

Robbins, Harvey and Michael Finley, *The New Why Teams Don't Work—What Goes Wrong and How to Make it Right.* San Francisco: Berrett-Koehler Publishers, Inc. 2000.

TRANSLATION TO THE LEADERSHIP ARCHITECT® COMPETENCY LIBRARY

In order for a team or individuals on a team to perform well in this area, these are the competencies that would most likely be in play. Aside from a team improvement plan where everybody works on the same thing, some individual team members may need to work on some of these competencies. A critical number (but not necessarily all) of team members would have to be good at:

MISSION CRITICAL:

- ☐ 42. Peer Relationships
- ☐ 51. Problem Solving
- ☐ 53. *Drive for* Results
- ☐ 60. *Building Effective* Teams

IMPORTANT:

- ☐ 12. Conflict Management
- ☐ 27. Informing
- ☐ 45. Personal Learning
- ☐ 50. Priority Setting
- ☐ 62. Time Management

NICE TO HAVE:

- ☐   7. Caring About Direct Reports
- ☐ 15. Customer Focus
- ☐ 36. Motivating Others
- ☐ 57. Standing Alone

In addition to the ten tips listed for this cluster, there are additional tips that may apply from *FYI For Your Improvement*™. Below are the four items from the TEAM ARCHITECT® that make up this cluster. The item number appears to the left of each item. Immediately below the text of each item are competency and tip numbers from *FYI*. The competency is listed first (from 1 to 67), followed by the tip number (1 to 10). For example, 33-4 refers to competency 33 (Listening), tip number 4. The tips are generally written for individual development so some adaptation might be needed in the team context.

  6. Team members sacrifice their own needs for the good of the team.

  40-1; 42-6; 50-3; 53-1; 60-1,5,6,9; 62-3,7

24. Little or no internal competition undermines team efforts.

  12-1,3; 27-2; 42-5; 51-1,3; 60-1,5,7; 63-1

41. Team members put effort into building team cohesion.

  36- 1,3,5; 42-1,7,8; 60-1,6,7; 110-4

60. When one person struggles, other team members are there to help.

  3-6; 10-6; 42-1,5; 53-2; 56-2,3; 60-3,8; 110-4

7

TALENT—The necessary collective skills to get the job done

Talent Acquisition and Enhancement—Was there sufficient talent on the team to get done what they needed to do?

UNSKILLED

☐ The team does not possess the necessary skills and talent to accomplish its mission

☐ The team is made up of people who fit the culture or fit the style preferences of the team, but not the skill requirements

☐ Team members do not upgrade their skills or retool their capabilities

☐ Team members do not provide much improvement feedback to each other

☐ Team may hire new members they know or are comfortable with, without following any procedures

☐ The team does not have measures in place to align skills and talent with its charter

☐ Team tries to get by with existing skills and may ignore its limitations

☐ The team has a strong "not invented here" viewpoint and will not ask for nor seek help outside the team to achieve its goals

☐ The team is slow to recognize the need to change

SKILLED (TEAM ARCHITECT® ITEMS WITH NUMBERS)

☐ (7) The team has systems in place to help its members gain the skills and information they need

☐ (25) Team members give each other positive and negative feedback to improve performance and team functioning

☐ (43) The team follows a recruiting and staffing process to ensure it has the range of talents necessary to achieve its goals

☐ (61) If the team has a knowledge or skill limitation, it faces it promptly and looks for help to fill the gap

☐ When the team has an opening to fill, it usually tries to get the best talent it can, even if the new member is better than existing members at some skills and talents

☐ The team has measures in place to help it align talent against its mission

☐ The team debriefs both successes and failures looking for opportunities for improvement

☐ The team is not hesitant to go outside to get the skills and talents it needs on a short-term basis

☐ Team members trust that critical feedback from other team members is given solely with the collective interest of improving

OVERUSED (TOO MUCH OF A GOOD THING)

☐ Team spends too much time cross-training or learning new skills that may not be mission critical

☐ Members exchange so much direct critical feedback that personal relationships have been damaged beyond repair

☐ Team is so rigid in following alignment staffing processes that they slow down adding people in time

☐ Team hires too many narrow experts to fill short-term technical needs at the expense of hiring members with more general or future skills

☐ Team spends too much time analyzing skill gaps and not acting on integrating skill resources

☐ Team goes outside so much for what it needs that internal development is stalled

Note on overused strengths: Strengths used too much or too singly tend to have the negative effects listed above. To decrease those negative consequences, you have two alternatives. You can scale down or use the strength less or you can compensate for it with another skill or behavior. In practice, it is very difficult to get an individual or a team to use a strength less. Therefore, the best path is to develop compensators. Below are listed other TEAM ARCHITECT® clusters that would compensate for overusing this dimension and compensating skills from the LEADERSHIP ARCHITECT® library of 67 competencies.

COMPENSATING TEAM CLUSTERS: 8, 13, 15, 16

COMPENSATING COMPETENCIES: 19, 31, 36, 53, 60

SOME CAUSES OF POOR PERFORMANCE

- ☐ Members may be arrogant; think they know it all
- ☐ Members don't know what they don't know
- ☐ Members are blocked learners
- ☐ Organization has poor training resources
- ☐ Organization has poor staffing resources
- ☐ Organization isn't focused on development
- ☐ Organization is not open with information and communication
- ☐ Organizational culture is too polite; doesn't give critical feedback
- ☐ Members avoid conflict
- ☐ Members may be defensive when given feedback
- ☐ Good old boy network rules staffing decisions
- ☐ Team has had too many changes in team membership
- ☐ Change has been so rapid that the team can't keep up

THE MAP

It doesn't get any more basic or self-evident than this. You can't be a high-performing team if the team does not collectively possess the skills that match the requirements of the task. Period. It doesn't matter if the team has set its sights on being first. It doesn't matter if it has laid out an elaborate plan to get there. It doesn't even matter if it has an enlightened leader. If it lacks the skills or a process to get them, it will not perform. On the other hand, having the skills on board does not guarantee winning. The team may be ill led. Unfocused. Badly situated in a nonsupportive culture. Or, the team members spend time competing inside the team for glory. So task one is to get the skills on board needed to achieve the mission and to have a process in place to keep the skills fresh as challenges shift.

SOME REMEDIES

☐ **1. Align task requirements and skills.** Every permanent or temporary team has a set of work challenges, issues, goals and objectives, stated or implied. Successfully performing against those requirements takes a certain mix of skills, styles and talents. As part of the chartering exercise, the team should list the challenges, issues, goals and objectives on one side of the chart, and then list the specific technical, functional, teaming and personal skills that will be necessary to effectively work against those tasks. That list of skills and talents can then be used for assessing skill gaps in the team, selecting new team members, assigning members to tasks, training programs for new skills, and acquiring outside resources where significant gaps exist.

☐ **2. Identify teaming skill requirements.** Identify the competencies needed to be a successful team member on this team at this time. Most of these teaming skills have already been identified through research and are contained in the TEAM ARCHITECT®. Also read *Team Players and Teamwork* by Glenn M. Parker to learn more. He has identified the following team-player skills: Planning and goal-setting, meeting management, listening, resolving conflict, consensus building, presentation skills, risk taking, problem solving, role clarification, mentorship, ethics, assertiveness and giving/receiving feedback among other things. Each team will have its own unique requirements based upon the stage of development it is in and what the tasks are that need to be accomplished. Publish the skill requirements so people understand where they fit and where they don't. This will help with the skills inventory that needs to occur.

☐ **3. Conduct a continuous skills inventory.** Once the teaming requirements have been identified, it is important to inventory the talent on the team to figure out what you have and what gaps might slow the team down. Boss, other team members and self should assess each team member. Use the results of the team skills inventory to prioritize training needs for individuals, the entire team and outside resource needs. In high-performing teams, the skills need to be in the team collectively, that is, not all team members need to be good at everything. This will be addressed later in Cluster 8, Talent Allocation/Deployment.

☐ **4. Use a disciplined recruiting process.** There are research based and experience tested best practices for selecting the people that best fit the needs of a position and a team. Those practices include structured interviewing on team competencies, multiple interviewers and a disciplined decision making process. *Select members based on skills and potential, not personalities.* The key issue for teams is striking the right balance between members who already possess the needed skill levels versus developing the skill levels after they join the team. Far too many leaders overemphasize selection of all skills up front. With the exception of some advanced technical or functional skills, many people can develop needed skills *after* selection. If the organization is willing to help the team members grow, selecting for potential may be the best bet. Hiring someone with all the skills will be difficult; hiring someone with many of the skills and a learning attitude is more productive. See the RECRUITING ARCHITECT® for more information on these practices.

☐ **5. Align training.** While initial selection is important to team performance, it is as important to foster the conditions after selection that allow members to continually develop and earn their membership in the team. Technical training and refinement might be available within the team. The organization should provide workshops designed to foster team-player skills and effective teamwork. The first step is a basic program in team-player styles and characteristics of an effective team, where team members learn to identify their team-player styles to increase their personal effectiveness. The workshop should also provide a framework to assess their current team against the twelve characteristics of an effective team and to develop a plan for improvement. Those twelve characteristics, identified by Glenn M. Parker are:

1. Clear purpose
2. Informality
3. Participation
4. Listening
5. Civilized disagreement
6. Consensus decisions
7. Open communications
8. Clear roles and work assignments
9. Shared leadership
10. External relations
11. Style diversity
12. Self-assessment

☐ **6. Give and ask for feedback.** If the team has established values early in the process, giving feedback was probably one of them. Have the team leader or coach facilitate a *preferred* feedback exercise. Have each team member identify how they prefer to give and receive feedback. Have them explain why that is their preference. Everyone isn't the same. Some people get their feelings hurt more than others. Some will get embarrassed. Some will fuss. Some will get mad and turn red. Create a matrix of the feedback preference results that members feel strongly about. Post the matrix and make sure everyone has a copy and follows the preferences if possible.

RECEIVING FEEDBACK PREFERENCES

	Face-to-Face	One-on-One	With the Team	Immediately	After a Cool-Down Period	Over e-mail	Other?
Joe	Always					Never	
Mary	Sometimes			Always		Sometimes	
Tim	Always		Never				

☐ **7. Follow feedback-giving guidelines.** Have the team review the following tips on how to give useful feedback:

■ *Be sensitive.* Give the feedback privately unless it calls for a group intervention, or unless you are in a group debrief/processing session.

■ *Be balanced.* Don't sandwich or sugarcoat the feedback but do mention some good things the person does that leaves him or her feeling resourceful and not beaten up.

■ *Be specific.* Try to avoid words like "usually" or "sometimes." Give specific examples with behaviors that were observed.

■ *Have courage.* Say what needs to be said. Don't hold back. Avoid a long preamble where the person hears nothing while waiting for the "bad news." "Here's where you can make a 3% improvement on your performance" is often all that needs to be said as an opener. This statement clearly implies that the person is competent, can improve and that this is not an 80% improvement situation.

■ *Own the feedback.* Avoid saying things like "I heard" or "the team thinks." If you are giving the feedback, say what *you* think, how *you* feel and what *you* saw or heard.

■ *Listen.* Give the person a chance to absorb your feedback and hear the other side of the story.

■ *Give direction.* Help the person process the situation. Ask how the situation could have been handled differently. Don't give all the answers. Let the person figure it out as much as possible.

■ *Keep it private.* If your intention is to help the person, keep the situation confidential.

☐ **8. Be a gracious feedback recipient.** Have the team work on receiving feedback. Receiving feedback is sometimes more difficult than giving it. Remember that it takes a lot of courage for a teammate to sit down and share some negative information. If you are a team member receiving feedback, consider the following tips:

- *Listen.* Have an open mind. Hear the person out. Don't let any biases you have toward the person giving feedback get in the way of hearing the message.

- *Be patient.* If you cut the person off, he or she will be less apt to help you in the future.

- *Manage non-verbals.* The signals you send off can speak louder than words. Make eye contact; don't roll your eyes; don't fold your arms, etc.

- *Stay composed.* It is normal to have feelings, but try to productively manage them. Don't shoot the messenger.

- *Don't get defensive.* Try not to explain yourself out of the situation or defend your actions if the messenger has a point.

- *Accept all feedback, even if it's wrong.* Now is not the time to point out that this view is incorrect. If on reflection and further counsel it is factually wrong, the question becomes why are you seen that way? Why would you see someone that way? Your goal will then be to devise a plan to present yourself as you are, and not engage in misleading behaviors.

- *Rephrase for clarity.* Repeat the message back that you are hearing to make sure you have it straight.

- *Apologize if necessary.* If remorse is warranted, show it. Don't let your arrogance or pride block it.

- *Identify a strategy for improvement.* Process what you could have done differently. Ask the messenger for input and agreement.

- *Ask for more feedback.* If you are willing to improve, ask the messenger to continue to observe you and give regular feedback on your progress (or lack thereof).

- *Thank the feedback giver.* This is true even if you are having trouble accepting the feedback.

☐ **9. Solicit outside expertise**. If the team has a knowledge or skill limitation, it needs to identify ways to fill the gap. Generally gaps will exist in highly technical or functional areas. If full-time membership is not warranted in these areas, consider ad-hoc members or part-time members or consultants. Invite these valuable contributors in when it makes sense.

☐ **10. Adjust to changes in team membership.** Read *Hot Groups—Seeding Them, Feeding Them & Using Them to Ignite Your Organization* by Jean Lipman-Blumen & Harold J. Leavitt. The book suggests that the loss of a valued team member can be painful and the loss of the team leader can even be fatal. High-performing teams are sometimes fragile. If forming has occurred and the team is mature and used to working with each other, it may not realize how much it really depends on one another until someone leaves. If the loss is due to an accepted, or planned manner, i.e., retirement, it is difficult, but the team can generally cope. However, if the loss is due to health problems, unexpected resignation, organizational politics, sabotage or defection, the effects can be serious. Here are some tips from the authors on treating changes in team membership:

- Look for signs of unexpected defections. Most departures have warning signals. If the team is forewarned, it can cope better.

- Try a radical organ transplant. Immediately replace the member. Realize that organ transplants many times don't work though, and may be rejected.

- Provide lots of support for the team. Have a facilitator help the team acknowledge the impact of the loss and target some strategies to get the group back on track.

- Let team members participate in and own re-staffing issues. If a team is truly high-performing, it has spent a lot of time forming, storming, and norming, and doesn't want to start all over again because of a change in team membership. High-performing teams may require slight "bends" in existing corporate staffing policies. Even though recruiting for a new member means some deviation from work, most high-performing teams would rather do it themselves.

SUGGESTED READINGS

Katzenbach, Jon R. and Douglas K. Smith, *The Wisdom of Teams.* New York: HarperCollins. 1993.

Lipman-Blumen, Jean and Harold J. Leavitt, *Hot Groups— Seeding Them, Feeding Them & Using Them to Ignite Your Organization.* New York: Oxford University Press, Inc. 1999.

Parker, Glenn M., *Team Players and Teamwork.* San Francisco: Jossey-Bass, Inc. 1990 & 1996.

TRANSLATION TO THE LEADERSHIP ARCHITECT® COMPETENCY LIBRARY

In order for a team or individuals on a team to perform well in this area, these are the competencies that would most likely be in play. Aside from a team improvement plan where everybody works on the same thing, some individual team members may need to work on some of these competencies. A critical number (but not necessarily all) of team members would have to be good at:

MISSION CRITICAL:

- ☐ 25. Hiring and Staffing
- ☐ 27. Informing
- ☐ 50. Priority Setting
- ☐ 51. Problem Solving
- ☐ 53. *Drive for* Results
- ☐ 56. Sizing Up People

IMPORTANT:

- ☐ 19. Developing People
- ☐ 39. Organizing Skills
- ☐ 62. Time Management

NICE TO HAVE:

- ☐   1. Action Oriented
- ☐ 12. Conflict Management
- ☐ 17. Decision Quality
- ☐ 18. Delegation
- ☐ 29. Integrity and Trust
- ☐ 34. Managerial Courage

In addition to the ten tips listed for this cluster, there are additional tips that may apply from *FYI For Your Improvement*™. Below are the four items from the TEAM ARCHITECT® that make up this cluster. The item number appears to the left of each item. Immediately below the text of each item are competency and tip numbers from *FYI*. The competency is listed first (from 1 to 67), followed by the tip number (1 to 10). For example, 33-4 refers to competency 33 (Listening), tip number 4. The tips are generally written for individual development so some adaptation might be needed in the team context.

7. The team has systems in place to help its members gain the skills and information they need.

    27-1,2,3,4,5,10; 39-5; 50-2; 52-3; 62-2

25. Team members give each other positive and negative feedback to improve performance and team functioning.

    12-7; 29-1,7,8; 34-1,2,3,7,8; 35-7

43. The team follows a recruiting and staffing process to ensure it has the range of talents necessary to achieve its goals.

    25-1,3,6,7,8; 53-1; 56-1,3,4,7

61. If the team has a knowledge or skill limitation, it faces it promptly and looks for help to fill the gap.

    1-1; 18-5,9; 25-1,6; 53-1; 56-4,5; 110-4,8

TALENT ACQUISITION AND ENHANCEMENT

7

69

8

TALENT ALLOCATION/DEPLOYMENT

TALENT—The necessary collective skills to get the job done

Talent Allocation/Deployment—Were the right people assigned to the right tasks?

UNSKILLED

☐ Team does not leverage all of the strengths of individual members

☐ Team allows individual shortcomings to stall team performance

☐ Individual team members compete for space and credit

☐ Team members are not aware of one another's strengths

☐ Team may have one or more members who are star performers

☐ Team may have one or more members who are poor performers

☐ Talent within the team is neither complementary nor balanced

☐ Team members do not have a clear idea about who is responsible for what; roles are not clear

☐ New members of the team are given the less desirable jobs

SKILLED (TEAM ARCHITECT® ITEMS WITH NUMBERS)

☐ (8) Team members readily defer to one another where the other is more skilled or knowledgeable in an area

☐ (26) Talent is viewed collectively; there is little or no individual competition

☐ (44) Each team member's strengths and weaknesses are known to all

☐ (62) Talent is reasonably balanced across the whole team; one or a few people do not dominate it

☐ Team has clarity on roles and responsibilities

☐ Team celebrates wins and victories even when all have not been involved

☐ Team is not worried about who does what; they are just interested in achieving the mission of the team

☐ Team members have no trouble delegating part of their job or role to others on the team

OVERUSED (TOO MUCH OF A GOOD THING)

☐ Team members are so good at using everyone else's strengths that other members do not develop new skills

☐ Team members are labeled due to strengths or weaknesses and can't overcome stereotypes associated with the labels

☐ Team becomes hesitant to let anyone try anything for the first time

☐ The team exchanges so much personal skill information that the mood gets too raw

☐ The team is so well oiled that it's hard for a new team member to fit in and get up-to-speed

☐ Team is so well balanced that no one stands out for promotion to the next level

☐ Team may have trouble competing outside the team since it tries so hard not to be competitive inside

Note on overused strengths: Strengths used too much or too singly tend to have the negative effects listed above. To decrease those negative consequences, you have two alternatives. You can scale down or use the strength less or you can compensate for it with another skill or behavior. In practice, it is very difficult to get an individual or a team to use a strength less. Therefore, the best path is to develop compensators. Below are listed other TEAM ARCHITECT® clusters that would compensate for overusing this dimension and compensating skills from the LEADERSHIP ARCHITECT® library of 67 competencies.

COMPENSATING TEAM CLUSTERS: 7, 10, 16, 18

COMPENSATING COMPETENCIES: 7, 19, 23, 31, 36

72

SOME CAUSES OF POOR PERFORMANCE

☐ Team may be very new and does not know each other well enough

☐ The team's tasks and specialties may not benefit much from cooperation

☐ The team's manager does not allow the team to work together much

☐ Members may be too stubborn or arrogant to defer work to others who have more expertise or capability

☐ Members may be overly ambitious

☐ Team has not conducted self or team skill assessments

☐ Members are not self-aware of their own strengths and weaknesses

☐ Members avoid conflict so they don't discuss skill limitations or gaps

☐ Team leader may not be good at sizing up others and allocating work

☐ Team staffs poorly; team clones skills they already have

☐ Team has not identified clear roles and responsibilities

THE MAP

A unique quality of a high-performing team is its ability and willingness to apply the strengths of individuals against key tasks, regardless of whose specific job it is. The best presenter presents in mission critical situations. The best analyst analyzes in situations where it has to be right. The best people judge manages the selection of new team members. Not all team members of a high-performing team need to be skilled in everything. In a well-functioning team, the real key is, does the team have all skill requirements covered collectively? High-performing teams bring together complementary skills and experiences that far exceed any individual on the team or the output of all the team members acting alone. It doesn't do any good to build a team with the right capabilities if the team doesn't deploy them collectively and effectively. Talent deployment requires, first, an understanding of capabilities (and liabilities) within the team, and then willingness and flexibility in using these individual skills collectively to achieve successful outcomes. That means team members have to share, step aside from time to time or step into the breach if needed.

SOME REMEDIES

☐ **1. Determine the skill requirements for the team.** The first step is to determine what the skill requirements are that will allow the team to accomplish its objectives. Have the team spend time looking at the issues and challenges that will be facing the team during the next time unit—usually a year. The team already has its charter from previous steps so the question is, what will the team face in trying to reach its goals in terms of:

- Economics
- Markets
- Labor market for talent
- Regulatory issues
- Competitor activity
- Environmental requirements
- Resources
- Political considerations
- Constituencies in the way
- Constituencies that could help
- Customer requirements
- Time frames
- Alliances needed

Once the issues and challenges are listed, derive the skills that will be needed to solve the challenge or face the issue. So if a challenge is getting several reluctant constituents on board, then key skills might be influencing and motivating others. If the issue is going to be tight time frames, then some key skills would be *Timely* Decision Making or Priority Setting. In addition or alternately, there is a Lominger tool called ORGANIZATIONAL CULTRIBUTE ARCHITECT® which can accomplish the same task. The outcome of either process is a list of the mission critical competencies the team must have in order to be successful.

☐ **2. Assign roles and work assignments.** One of the best ways to get members to defer to one another is to identify clear roles. This may be done by developing a job description for each member with a series of tasks listed. The concept of *role* goes beyond listing tasks for each team member. Effective teamwork involves task interdependence, so agreement on team roles and responsibilities is very important. Here are some tips to building clear roles:

- **Break the work to be done down into tasks.**

- **Define shared responsibilities.** Which tasks cannot be done by individuals alone?

- **Define individual responsibilities.** Have members exchange input on each role. Team effectiveness is optimized when members know what others expect of them or understand why there is a conflict in expectations.

- **Identify the importance of each role.** Many team conflicts are actually substantive and often related to roles or procedures.

- **Revisit role clarification often.** Especially when 1) there is role conflict or ambiguity, 2) a new team is forming, or 3) a new member joins the team.

It is important to know that lack of role clarity can derail a team's success. Role conflict and ambiguity can cause considerable stress on a team and result in lost productivity, dissatisfaction and a tendency of members to leave the team.

☐ **3. Discover strengths and weaknesses within the team.** There are many options for skill assessment. Self-assessment is an OK starting place, but input from others is the best source for real assessment data. You can do a formal 360° assessment process of the mission critical skills identified in Tip 1. Each individual would get a report. Each individual would have a development plan. Then the individual reports would be rolled up into a group report. Have the team work the group report to locate common strengths and weaknesses. Then have the team create a group development plan, a plan everyone would work on. Or have a coach facilitate a live feedback process for each member. This will increase the awareness of capability within the team, help each member direct his or her own development, and decrease defensive reactions to feedback in the future. This process will work best after the team has been in place for several months so that members have had firsthand experience in observing behaviors within the team.

- Establish ground rules for the feedback process up front to be sensitive and respectful of member's feelings. Then explain the three rules: 1) State things positively, 2) Be behaviorally specific, and 3) Leave the member in an action state (offer specific ways to improve).

- Team member to receive the feedback leaves the room.

- Coach/facilitator explains to the team that they will be making four lists in response to these questions:
  1. What does the member do well that you want him or her to continue doing?
  2. What does the member do that you don't like and want him or her to discontinue doing?
  3. What does the member not do, that you would want him or her to begin doing?
  4. What questions do you want the member to answer?

- Facilitator has written these four questions on separate flipchart sheets and arranged them around the room. Facilitator leads the discussion, elicits responses and records them on the flipchart paper.

- The team takes a break while the facilitator goes over the flipchart information individually with the member who was discussed.

- The team reconvenes with the member and the facilitator present. The member comments on and explains him or herself in response to the flipchart information. He or she may ask questions to the team to get more specific feedback. The member thanks the team for participating in the exercise.

- The facilitator provides a written summary of the flipchart information to the member for future development reference.

- The member incorporates this information and suggestions into his or her style and development plan.

- Repeat this process for other team members and the leader.

Another way to do the same process is to give everyone in the room four colors of index cards. Assign a color to:

1. Things you think the team member should keep doing
2. Things you think the team member should stop doing
3. Things you think the team member should start doing
4. Things you think the team member should keep doing but modify a bit

Each member of the team writes four cards—one of each color—for each member of the team. When everyone is finished, the cards are delivered to each member. In a 10-person team, each member would get 40 cards. Have each member review the material and then follow the process outlined above. The end product is a development plan for everyone on the team.

☐ **4. Allow all individuals to contribute.** Performing teams always find ways for each individual to contribute and thereby gain distinction. If the team purpose or goal calls for output that certain individual members are best suited for, let them perform. This will require some members on the team to step back from time to time and let their peer(s) shine. High-performing teams know that certain situations may call for expertise and speed to get the needed performance results.

☐ **5. Talent mix and balance.** According to Glenn M. Parker, author of *Team Players and Teamwork*, the most effective teams must have a balance of team-player styles. Pages 155-163 of his book can help team members determine where they fit in to balance team effectiveness.

Style	Description
Contributor	Task-oriented—Completing their work in a high-quality manner.
Collaborator	Goal-oriented—Reaching their goals with a strong commitment.
Communicator	Process-oriented—Developing and maintaining a positive team climate.
Challenger	Question-oriented—Raising questions about the team's goals and methods.

Effective teams know that having balance does not mean equal use of all styles at all times. Balance means having the capability to use the various styles when required. Missing a role or two can cause trouble, as can all of one style. A team's need for a particular style is situational, and often based on the stage of team development.

☐ **6. Address talent imbalances.** There are several types of talent imbalances on teams:

- One or more members are star performers.
- One or more members are poor performers.
- One or more members may be dominating or bullying the team.
- Member styles are too similar.
- Needed style may be lacking.

Once the imbalance is found, possible solutions include:

- Aggressively coaching laggard performers.
- Confronting dominating or bullying team members. Revisit team values and discuss the implications on other members.
- Removing poor performers from the team.
- Adding members who fill talent or style gaps.

Understand potential pitfalls of not addressing talent imbalances:

- Workload may become unbalanced as a result of talent differences.
- Star performers will resent poor performers for their lack of contribution.
- Poor performers may resent star performers for getting all the recognition.
- Star performers may leave.
- Poor performers may eventually give up and coast or let others carry the load.

☐ **7. Distribute bad jobs**. One potential pitfall of deferring to skill or expertise within in the team is the possibility that one or more members may continually inherit the "bad jobs." These are generally undesirable assignments. They could be

78

team paperwork, monthly reporting, housekeeping, etc. Here are a few tips to deal with that situation:

■ **Get rid of bad jobs.** Having the same people always do the bad jobs creates tension and inequality in the team. If you cannot eliminate these jobs, consider contracting them out.

■ **Rotate them.** If bad jobs can't be taken out of a team, consider rotating them. Create a visual on a poster that lists a schedule or rotation of team members assigned to the bad jobs. Everyone on the team must pull his or her fair share of unappetizing work if the team is to succeed.

■ **Speak up.** If you are a team member who is frustrated because you feel like you always get the bad jobs, say something about it.

☐ **8. Address turf wars.** Just like as there are bad jobs, there are also jobs that members perceive to be glory jobs. Problems often occur when one person on a team has responsibility for a single (usually appealing) task. This happens often **on cross-functional or senior management teams.** When two parties perceive a task as their turf, they can be prepared to violate the spirit of collaboration to ensure the turf remains theirs. Conflict and team noise occurs when members perceive the turf issue to represent power for them (or lack thereof). Turf wars can mean trouble for a team. Here are some tips to overcome turf wars:

■ Negotiate specific tasks.

■ Agree on procedures to update team members on progress.

■ Collaborate with team members who have a vested interest.

■ Assign clear accountabilities for results (to avoid later blame).

☐ **9. Think transcompetition.** The book *The New Why Teams Don't Work—What Goes Wrong and How to Make It Right* suggests that there is no such thing as friendly competition, primarily because it is a win or lose proposition. Similarly, too much collaboration within a team can leave it weak, slow and not likely to change. Rather, *transcompetition* is a combination of collaboration and competition. Find ways to marry the two for team success.

8

Competition/ Collaboration	How to Apply
The will to greatness vs. the will to commonality	Leverage ambition to achieve great things, but do it with a balance to survive when we screw up. Look for win/win situations. Understand that some people are born with talent, but most struggle to attain it.
Focus vs. empathy	Focus on the task, but continue to scan the environment to understand from the outside in. Focus is about me. Empathy is about us. Teams require both.
Persistence vs. insistence	Persistence is heroic, the willingness to die for a cause. Insistence is about survival in order to keep the cause alive. Teams need star performance but they also need pluggers who show up every day and do the work that needs doing.
Results vs. process	It's the what and how. They must be balanced.
Play vs. work	Play is a team's genius—its ability to generate, innovate, revolutionize from thin air. Work is why we show up and don't feel so playful. Transcompetition means abandoning the pain principle for the pleasure principle: Work for the fun of it.
Personalization vs. depersonalization	Personalization allows for customization and feeling. Depersonalization is detachment and an ability to see a thing without regard to its effect on you. When detachment comes in, out goes paranoia, disrespect, and the blind-ness that often accompanies self-interest.
Loose vs. tight	Determine whether structures and relationships call for bonds that need tightened for success or if a loose approach will encourage free minds to find solutions.

☐ **10. Celebrate Wins as a Team.** No matter who does what, celebrate as a team. If everyone on the team is dedicated to collective success and is willing to either take or defer tasks for the benefit of the team, then it follows that all successes and wins belong to everyone. Have parties, surprises with ice cream, team dress on special occasions, roast each other after work, come up with team code phrases and symbols. Whatever would be fun for the team, do it.

SUGGESTED READINGS

Fisher, Kimball, Steven Rayner, William Belgard and the Belgard-Fisher-Rayner Team. *Tips for Teams: A Ready Reference for Solving Common Team Problems.* New York: McGraw-Hill, Inc. 1995.

Katzenbach, Jon R. and Douglas K.Smith, *The Wisdom of Teams.* New York: HarperCollins. 1993.

Parker, Glenn M., *Team Players and Teamwork.* San Francisco: Jossey-Bass, Inc. 1990 & 1996.

Robbins, Harvey and Michael Finley, *The New Why Teams Don't Work—What Goes Wrong and How to Make it Right.* San Francisco: Berrett-Koehler Publishers, Inc. 2000.

TRANSLATION TO THE LEADERSHIP ARCHITECT® COMPETENCY LIBRARY

In order for a team or individuals on a team to perform well in this area, these are the competencies that would most likely be in play. Aside from a team improvement plan where everybody works on the same thing, some individual team members may need to work on some of these competencies. A critical number (but not necessarily all) of team members would have to be good at:

MISSION CRITICAL:

☐ 44. Personal Disclosure

☐ 55. Self-knowledge

☐ 56. Sizing Up People

☐ 60. *Building Effective* Teams

IMPORTANT:

☐ 12. Conflict Management

☐ 18. Delegation

☐ 53. *Drive for* Results

NICE TO HAVE:

☐ 25. Hiring and Staffing

☐ 39. Organizing

☐ 40. *Dealing with* Paradox

☐ 42. Peer Relationships

In addition to the ten tips listed for this cluster, there are additional tips that may apply from *FYI For Your Improvement*™. Below are the four items from the TEAM ARCHITECT® that make up this cluster. The item number appears to the left of each item. Immediately below the text of each item are competency and tip numbers from *FYI*. The competency is listed first (from 1 to 67), followed by the tip number (1 to 10). For example, 33-4 refers to competency 33 (Listening), tip number 4. The tips are generally written for individual development so some adaptation might be needed in the team context.

8. Team members readily defer to one another where the other is more skilled or knowledgeable in an area.

    18-5,9; 55-1,3,5; 56-2,3,4; 60-8,10

26. Talent is viewed collectively; there is little or no individual competition.

    12-1; 23-5; 27-3; 42-5; 60-1,6,8; 110-2,4,6

44. Each team member's strengths and weaknesses are known to all.

    31-5; 44-1,6,7; 55-1,3; 56-2,3,5; 60-8

62. Talent is reasonably balanced across the whole team; one or a few people do not dominate it.

    25-1,3,6,7,8; 56-1,3,4,7; 60-8

9

TEAMING SKILLS—Operating the team's business efficiently and effectively

Resource Management—Was the team short on resources? Did the team waste resources? Did the team spin its wheels? Did the team go outside for resources or best practices?

UNSKILLED

☐ Team spends time on unimportant things

☐ Team is not productive when working together

☐ Team members complain about spinning wheels but don't do anything to get traction

☐ Team is very internally or "not invented here" focused; doesn't look for or ask for external resources

☐ Team is disorganized with approach, assignments and resources

☐ Members do not leverage previous experiences as learnings that improve future team performance

☐ The team has to do a lot of rework on things that were not done right in the first place

☐ It's hard to find the team member you need to obtain resources that team member controls

SKILLED (TEAM ARCHITECT® ITEMS WITH NUMBERS)

☐ (9) Team members use their experiences to strengthen how the team operates

☐ (27) The team uses time well (in meetings, on assignments); there is little wasted motion

☐ (45) The team is not afraid to ask for and use outside help

☐ (63) The team organizes and uses its resources efficiently

- [ ] This team gets more done with less compared to other teams
- [ ] Most events come off on time and on schedule in the team
- [ ] It's easy to find the resources you need when you need them even when they are controlled and managed by another team member
- [ ] The team is successful making its case for the need for additional resources

OVERUSED (TOO MUCH OF A GOOD THING)

- [ ] Team members are too focused on the tried and true, thereby limiting creativity and experimentation
- [ ] Team is so structured with time that they become inflexible and lack spontaneity
- [ ] Team outsources too much, stifling internal opportunities for development
- [ ] Everything is run so tight that there is hardly any room or time to relax and enjoy the work
- [ ] Everything is so structured that there is little time for reflection and looking for unscheduled opportunities for adding value
- [ ] Team is held in such esteem that there is little time for rapport-building and social conversation when the time comes to get together

Note on overused strengths: Strengths used too much or too singly tend to have the negative effects listed above. To decrease those negative consequences, you have two alternatives. You can scale down or use the strength less or you can compensate for it with another skill or behavior. In practice, it is very difficult to get an individual or a team to use a strength less. Therefore, the best path is to develop compensators. Below are listed other TEAM ARCHITECT® clusters that would compensate for overusing this dimension and compensating skills from the LEADERSHIP ARCHITECT® library of 67 competencies.

COMPENSATING TEAM CLUSTERS: 10, 13, 14

COMPENSATING COMPETENCIES: 14, 19, 28, 32, 60

SOME CAUSES OF POOR PERFORMANCE

- ☐ Some team members may be blocked learners
- ☐ Team members may be disorganized
- ☐ Team members may be arrogant
- ☐ Team members may not be good time managers
- ☐ Team members may have narrow experiences
- ☐ Team members may not be focused on results
- ☐ Some members may be rigid
- ☐ Team members may not be resourceful
- ☐ Team members may be uncomfortable with uncertainty
- ☐ Team members may not follow through on commitments
- ☐ Team members may prefer to avoid conflict
- ☐ Team is impulsive and reactive

THE MAP

High-performing teams effectively manage their resources to achieve goals. These resources include people, skills, time, money, influence, etc. Managing resources requires the ability to juggle multiple tasks, organize things into sensible solutions and, most of all, executional discipline from team members. The key is doing more with less or getting more value per pound of resource than other teams.

SOME REMEDIES

- ☐ **1. Get organized.** Plan the work and then work the plan. Who on the team is best at organizing people and things? Put that person in charge of managing the team's budget, meeting agendas and things that require discipline, priority setting and follow-up. Not everyone has an eye for detail or can juggle multiple things at once. Disorganization can impede a team's productivity. Does the team have a resource allocation plan? Does the team have anyone good at basic planning? If not, send a willing member to a project management class to learn how to create and maintain a plan with planning software. Make resource management a priority for the team so that efficiency and organization are at the forefront of all activities. *More help? See FYI For Your Improvement, Chapter 39—Organizing and Chapter 47—Planning.*

☐ **2. Share leadership.** If members leave team meetings complaining that their time together was not fully utilized, ask them to say something about that at the next meeting when it counts. It is your team, your meeting, your valuable time, and therefore, your responsibility to do whatever it takes (for example, ask the group to stick to the agenda) to help ensure it is not a waste of time. Don't depend totally on the team leader to assume this role all of the time. He or she may be unaware that there is a problem. Leadership doesn't have to be assumed by the person with the position power, in this case, the team leader. Leadership is any action that helps a team to reach its goals. In successful teams, task and process leadership are shared and shift among team members, depending on the needs of the group and the skills of members.

There are two types of shared leadership responsibilities:

- Task Responsibilities—Actions that help the team reach its goals, accomplish an immediate task, make a decision, or solve a problem (time management, meeting planning, goal-setting, etc.).

- Process Responsibilities—How we go about accomplishing our task. In many cases, the process is interpersonal.

Identify opportunities to share leadership and to reinforce positive examples of the supporting leadership behaviors within the team. To learn more about shared leadership in teams, read *Team Players and Teamwork* by Glenn M. Parker.

☐ **3. Should the team be a team?** When the team meets, does the discussion content feel like a waste of time for all but a few in the room? Are some people bored in the meetings? Are meetings unproductive? If so, maybe the team shouldn't be a team on every task and every issue. Maybe the group is really just a bunch of people who report to the same boss, share common workspace and don't have much more than that in common. Ask the following questions:

RESOURCE MANAGEMENT

9

- Are the major relationships of the team members with each other or primarily with customers and technology? If the answer is the latter, the team may not really be a team.

- Is there opportunity for a group to set and enforce productivity or quality norms or is the work self-contained, repetitive and requires a high level of manual skill? If the answer is the latter, the team may not really be a team.

Bottom line: Teams only pay off when there are critical interdependencies that a team can manage and thereby add value to the organization. If working together doesn't add value, then team meetings may not add much. If the team really isn't a team, call it something else and quit pretending.

☐ **4. Ask for resources.** Learn to speak up to lobby for team needs. Ask for help obtaining the amount of human and monetary resources needed by the team to achieve its goals. You may not get it, but you'll have tried. Who is best at constructing the case? Who on the team is best at stating the case? What type of argument works best to those with resource authority? Results? Outcomes? Innovation? Customer satisfaction? Create a compelling case to inspire the resource providers. Paint a vivid picture of what results these resources will bring. High-performing teams are, in a sense, self-renewing because great results are usually followed by a larger share of the resources next cycle.

☐ **5. Beware of dwindling resources.** When teams have sizable goals, they can become a major consumer of resources. Long projects cost big money and require different types of organizational support. Generally, when an organization charters a team for a significant cause, it will also charter money. However, when a **project team's** funding rolls into following budget years, or when **cross-functional teams** lose a key sponsor, things can change. Resource support can also strangely change as a result of a team achieving lots of success. While it's just as true that resources go to the successful, success of the team can cause resentment in other parts of the organization. Competition and jealousy can spark sabotage against a high-performing team. Resource reduction is a quick and easy target. When a team's resources dwindle under the guise that the team doesn't need the degree of help other teams do, the team may begin to falter and become discouraged. Most high-performing teams will persevere and not give up; however, a cut in resources could sink an average team. In sum, keep an eye on resources, especially if they are at risk. Make sure the team is aligned with the right sponsors and support arms to maintain its resources. Have your case ready to go and be prepared to repeat it.

☐ **6. Conduct an experience audit.** Use the CAREER ARCHITECT® Expert System to conduct experience profiles for each team member. Identify the types of experiences each team member has had throughout their career (both on and off work experiences) to project which competencies they should have developed along the way. Compare those competencies to the team member profile and identify matches and gaps for each team member. Have each member receive 360° feedback (such as VOICES®) to validate competency proficiency. Team members may have had some experiences via development in current job assignments, off work or full time jobs that have fostered the growth of certain competencies that are critical for success in the team environment. Utilize your HR partner or team coach to help each member identify how they can apply the lessons of experience from the past to current challenges facing the team.

☐ **7. Work on the three big resource-eaters.** Studies on how teams work have shown three typical places where teams waste time and resources. These are meetings, decision making and down process time. Basically, meetings break down if there is no agenda, airtime is not managed, and topics are not closed. In typical meetings, some talk too much and some talk too little. In the studies, the amount of airtime did not predict the quality of the input. Have the team work on two skills. The first is how to convey the maximum or essential amount of information in the least amount of time. Limit statements from team members to a frequency and time limit. Also encourage those who usually do not speak up to do so. Many times they have a perspective that would move the process ahead. One common technique is to have each agenda item managed by a team member **who is not involved** in the item or its outcome. That item manager sets the rules, manages airtime and tries to move the item to resolution. The same technique can be used for making decisions. Each decision has a decision manager who moves the decision through the process as quickly and fairly as possible. Studies of decision making show that decisions lie quiet 85% of the time. No one is thinking about it and no one is working it. It is between inboxes or at the bottom of the pile of a key player in the decision making process. The task of the decision managers is to walk the decision through the steps so downtime is limited. When discussion ensues, research indicates that in effective problem solving groups, few people speak for longer than one minute. This gets people to make points, stick to issues and move the discussion along briskly.

☐ **8. Not-on-time teams.** Another time waster is organization cultures where meetings don't start on time. Usually one or two members of the team are always late. They are helter-skelter people who jump from one crisis to another. One person being late wastes the time of everyone else who was on time. Being late to a meeting signals a lack of respect for other team members. It is saying I am so important and the things I am doing are so important that I can't give up my valuable time for you. Aside from all agreeing to be on time, some teams use a fun fine or penalty system that everybody agrees with. It's like the bad language jar. If a team member is late for a meeting, they pay a fine for their tardiness based upon unexcused minutes. The money is donated to a favorite charity or used toward a team party at the end of the year. Have team members applaud when late members show up, then collect their fine on the spot. They'll get the message. Just remember to be sensitive when using this approach so as to not badger or embarrass someone who might have a legitimate reason for being late.

☐ **9. Honing team processes.** Using techniques like Total Quality Management, Process Reengineering or ISO, always work on trimming the time it takes to get things done. Make it a team goal to take steps out of processes. To do things in a shorter period of time. To use fewer resources per process step. To clarify the steps of all processes. To train new members quickly.

☐ **10. Manage meeting sickness.** Since meetings are such time wasters, have fewer meetings. If it's not to share critical information, solve an immediate problem, or alert people to changing trends and long-term problems that require study and follow-up, don't have a meeting at all. Make the meetings last different amounts of time given the topic at hand. Pick a no meeting day or two. This is a day people can depend on to be able to get their own things done. Depending upon travel patterns of the group, pick meeting days that allow the maximum flexibility for travel requirements. If there are no Monday meetings, people can schedule Sunday night travel to be at critical places early Monday mornings. If there is international travel, take time zone changes into consideration. For key meetings with heavy and hot topics, schedule meetings before international travel instead of after, when people are readjusting their body clocks. Beware of early morning staff meetings. While it's true most executives and managers are early birds and are clear headed at 7:30 AM, at least some are night owls and will not be at their best. In general, don't let meetings take up too much time of the team. Try to get by with the fewest meetings possible to get the work done. Another way to effectively manage team time and to deal with team members who are late for meetings is to meet at the same time for every team meeting. This approach can be used for daily, weekly, monthly or quarterly meetings. Starting at the same time will soon become easier for all team members to remember so that using the time becomes habit. If possible, use the same room so the team doesn't wonder where the meeting is being held. The team leader should always set an example for promptness. If abuse of time becomes an issue, revisit the team values to ensure that team members are respectful of each other's time, which can often be the scarcest resource.

SUGGESTED READINGS

Fisher, Kimball, Steven Rayner, William Belgard, and the Belgard-Fisher-Rayner Team. *Tips for Teams: A Ready Reference for Solving Common Team Problems.* New York: McGraw-Hill, Inc. 1995.

Lawler, Edward E. III, *From the Ground Up.* San Francisco: Jossey-Bass, Inc. 1996.

Lipman-Blumen, Jean and Harold J. Leavitt, *Hot Groups— Seeding Them, Feeding Them & Using Them to Ignite Your Organization.* New York: Oxford University Press, Inc. 1999.

Parker, Glenn M., *Team Players and Teamwork.* San Francisco: Jossey-Bass, Inc. 1990 & 1996.

Robbins, Harvey and Michael Finley, *The New Why Teams Don't Work—What Goes Wrong and How to Make it Right.* San Francisco: Berrett-Koehler Publishers, Inc. 2000.

TRANSLATION TO THE LEADERSHIP ARCHITECT® COMPETENCY LIBRARY

In order for a team or individuals on a team to perform well in this area, these are the competencies that would most likely be in play. Aside from a team improvement plan where everybody works on the same thing, some individual team members may need to work on some of these competencies. A critical number (but not necessarily all) of team members would have to be good at:

MISSION CRITICAL:

☐ 39. Organizing

☐ 50. Priority Setting

☐ 51. Problem Solving

☐ 52. Process Management

IMPORTANT:

☐ 47. Planning

☐ 53. *Drive for* Results

☐ 62. Time Management

NICE TO HAVE:

☐ 37. Negotiating

☐ 38. Organizational Agility

☐ 63. TQM/Reengineering

In addition to the ten tips listed for this cluster, there are additional tips that may apply from *FYI For Your Improvement*™. Below are the four items from the TEAM ARCHITECT® that make up this cluster. The item number appears to the left of each item. Immediately below the text of each item are competency and tip numbers from *FYI*. The competency is listed first (from 1 to 67), followed by the tip number (1 to 10). For example, 33-4 refers to competency 33 (Listening), tip number 4. The tips are generally written for individual development so some adaptation might be needed in the team context.

9. Team members use their experiences to strengthen how the team operates.

   24-10; 32-1,2,3; 51-3,8; 52-2,3; 63-2,6

27. The team uses time well (in meetings, on assignments); there is little wasted motion.

   50-1,3,7,9; 52-3,7,8; 62-1,3,10

45. The team is not afraid to ask for and use outside help.

   37-1,4; 38-3,4,8; 39-2; 42-1,5; 51-5; 53-6

63. The team organizes and uses its resources efficiently.

   39-1,2,6; 47-6,7; 50-2,3; 52-3,5; 53-3

10

TEAMING SKILLS—Operating the team's business efficiently and effectively

Team Learning—Did the team improve by learning from its successes and failures and the successes and failures of others?

UNSKILLED

- ☐ The team makes the same mistakes over and over again; no learning occurs
- ☐ The team tries to apply the same strengths to every situation
- ☐ Individual team members are not enhancing their skills or growing from their experience on the team
- ☐ The team does not make time for development and learning
- ☐ Some team members are stuck in their ways of doing things
- ☐ The team may not leverage new technology to improve its processes
- ☐ The team is often surprised by noisy events and unanticipated roadblocks
- ☐ The team attributes successes to itself and failures to others

SKILLED (TEAM ARCHITECT® ITEMS WITH NUMBERS)

- ☐ (10) The team debriefs its successes in order to find "repeatables" and perform better
- ☐ (28) The team debriefs its failures and mistakes in order to perform better
- ☐ (46) The team practices continuous improvement; team members are more skilled than they were a year ago
- ☐ (64) Team members are receptive to innovative approaches and new technology to improve its effectiveness

☐ The team has put in place a set of practices that keep it up-to-date

☐ The team makes learning new skills a priority

☐ The team constantly projects ahead to anticipate the opportunities and the potholes

☐ The team is open to learning from others inside the organization and adopting best practices that were not created in the team

☐ The team gets rid of the "old" to make room for the "new"

OVERUSED (TOO MUCH OF A GOOD THING)

☐ Team spends so much time reviewing their successes that they develop a false sense of security

☐ Team debriefs failures to such an extent that it de-motivates individuals on the team

☐ Team is always trying to reinvent processes at the expense of keeping an eye on results

☐ Team tries too many new approaches and leaves others in the organization behind

☐ Team casts out the old and the past too readily

☐ Team's advanced technology may not be compatible with the rest of the organization

☐ Team gets easily bored when things don't change fast enough

☐ Team spends too much time on skill development that is too far out in time to do any good

Note on overused strengths: Strengths used too much or too singly tend to have the negative effects listed above. To decrease those negative consequences, you have two alternatives. You can scale down or use the strength less or you can compensate for it with another skill or behavior. In practice, it is very difficult to get an individual or a team to use a strength less. Therefore, the best path is to develop compensators. Below are listed other TEAM ARCHITECT® clusters that would compensate for overusing this dimension and compensating skills from the LEADERSHIP ARCHITECT® library of 67 competencies.

COMPENSATING TEAM CLUSTERS: 1, 14, 15, 17, 18

COMPENSATING COMPETENCIES: 7, 23, 36, 38, 41, 48, 50

SOME CAUSES OF POOR PERFORMANCE

☐ Team members may be arrogant

☐ Team members may lack the self-confidence to explore and experiment with the new

☐ Some members may be blocked learners

☐ Team members may be uncomfortable with change; can't deal with uncertainty and ambiguity

☐ Team may not manage time well

☐ Team may be overextended

☐ Organization surrounding the team may not value learning or development

☐ Team leader does not model or recognize continuous learning

THE MAP

Change. It's the only constant. It's the only thing that stays the same. Few teams will be successful next year if they do exactly what they did last year this year. Markets are changing. Technology is changing. Competition is changing. We are all moving toward the global enterprise. Customer requirements are shifting. At one time, two-week photo processing was the norm. Then overnight. Then one hour. Now instant digital. Organizations, teams and individuals have to keep up. Teams have to scan ahead to check for performance-chilling changes. Teams have to set aside valuable time to get prepared for the anticipated future. Teams have to have a process and a culture in place that supports skill enhancement, process improvement and best practices or its performance will inevitably degrade.

SOME REMEDIES

☐ **1. Strengthen team learning capacity.** There are countless ways to improve your learning acumen as a team. Study two competitors, look at similar situations where teams succeeded and failed and figure out some guiding principles, storyboard (represent with pictures) a complex process so it is

TEAM LEARNING

10

easier to visualize, have team members study a new trend or technology and present it to the team, set up a competition with another group or find a team that faces similar problems to yours and use each other as consultants. If speed is your problem, practice quick experiments. Start small, try lots of things, make decisions quickly. Many problem solving studies show that it's the second or third time through before we really understand the dynamics of the problem we're working on. The more times you cycle through a problem, the more feedback, and the more opportunity to learn. *More help? See FYI For Your Improvement™, Chapter 28—Innovation Management and Chapter 32—Learning on the Fly.* Use the Lominger tool, the COMPABILITY ARCHITECT®, for a thorough assessment of your team's competencies and capabilities. Use the gaps identified to build team-learning enhancement plans to strengthen the learning capacity and speed of your team. High-performing teams regularly translate long-term purposes into definable performance goals and then develop the skills needed to meet those goals. As a result of doing this repeatedly, learning not only occurs once, it endures.

☐ **2. Strengthen individual learning capacities.** Teams won't do well if their members can't get outside the box. Following are some tips on increasing individual learning:

■ Throw out past solutions to a problem, even though they may have worked for you. Come up with something different by freewheeling it and allowing no evaluation of the ideas initially.

■ Look for parallels in other organizations and other fields. Don't be too local—ask the broader question. If your problem is poor order processing, ask who is the absolute best in this area? None of the likely answers such as Pizza Hut or Motorola may be in your direct business.

■ Pick out some interesting anomalies—facts that don't fit, like sales going down when they should have gone up, and ask what this might indicate.

■ Turn a problem upside down—ask what is the least likely cause of it, what the problem is not, or what the mirror image of the problem is.

- Ask more questions. Studies of problem solving groups show only about 7% of comments are questions.

- If something works, ask why until you are sure you have found something that is repeatable.

- Look for patterns in your successes and failures. What is common in each success? What is never present in a failure? What is always present in a failure but never present in a success?

More help? See FYI For Your Improvement, Chapter 14— Creativity. Use the LEARNING ARCHITECT® Development Tool Set to help individuals learn how to learn more effectively. The tool is comprised of several elements:

- LEARNING TACTICS™ helps people discover how they learn, specifically the tactics used most and least.

- LEARNING PROFILE™ lets people assess how active their methods and preferences for learning are. They find out if they are active, passive or blocked learners.

- LEARNING SKILLS™ helps people increase their least used learning skills.

- LEARNING DEFAULT (TROUBLESHOOTING)™ helps people spot the ways they may get in trouble under stress.

- LEARNING TIPS™ helps people create a Learning Enhancement Plan to address specific learning issues.

For a more formal assessment of learning acumen, eCHOICES® measures each individual's willingness and skill in learning new things and comfortably embracing change. Completed by the boss, colleagues and peers, the output contains a detailed report on the individual's learning strengths and weaknesses which have been related to current performance and future potential. You can use the tool, person by person, in which case an individual learning enhancement plan is constructed. If everyone on the team completes eCHOICES®, then a group report can be constructed with a group learning enhancement plan.

10

TEAM LEARNING

☐ **3. Define problems more thoroughly.** Most of us do a poor job of defining problems. We assume we know what it is, spend a minute or two on it at most, then leap in with numerous solutions. Argument and discussion then follow until something is selected, often the solution with the most vocal support. These instant and early conclusions lead to safe, historical solutions which may attack the wrong problem. High-performing teams don't do this—they devote much time, sometimes as much as 50% of the discussion, to the nature of the problem. To do this:

■ Ask what the problem is and what it isn't

■ See how many causes you can come up with

■ Organize the causes into themes or patterns

■ Don't suggest any solutions, just keep asking why this would happen or why this would not happen

☐ **4. Debrief team successes and failures.** A simple debriefing process can help to facilitate both open communication and learning. The process can also elicit both good and bad feedback about the team, its work processes and individual contributions. This type of group debrief helps create a comfortable environment where feedback is OK. Have the team leader, a coach or a facilitator ask and flipchart answers to the following questions after a key accomplishment or setback:

■ What went well?

■ What would we have done differently?

■ What did we learn?

■ How can we apply that learning?

Before jumping into the exercise, establish ground rules to be used during the discussion (i.e., all comments will be presented as constructively as possible, or members will share all thoughts and not withhold feelings, etc.). Also, make sure each member contributes at least one response to each of the questions. Use the learning for future challenges or situations that might be similar so as to not make the same mistakes twice.

In the case of debriefing successes, it's important for the team to honestly distinguish between things it did that directly contributed to success from those things that were windfall. Successful teams own up to the parts of success that were due to others and to circumstances not related directly to what they did. Lower performing teams take credit for everything and move on.

☐ **5. Encourage experimentation.** Experimenting always leads to a higher mistake exposure. Mistakes are good if we learn from them. Some of the greatest lessons in life, in work and in play, are learned from hardships. If the team is experimenting and looking for better, bigger, faster ways to do things, they will most likely make some mistakes along the way. It's quite OK, as long as it is in search of performance, getting results, experimenting and taking risks. Consider a few rules of thumb when it comes to making mistakes:

■ Was there a decent chance for success? Did the team analyze the idea or approach? You can minimize the impact or loss associated with a mistake by asking: "What is the worst thing that could happen if the team fails?" Dig deep when problem solving to find out if the team's idea has ever been tried before. If so, what was the result? Is your team's idea or approach better? Can you measure it to know if the team has achieved success?

■ Make different mistakes. If the team makes the same mistake twice, or even three times, there is a problem. The whole point of saying that experimenting and mistakes are OK is the assumption that learning occurs as a result. So figure out what went wrong and why. Was it an organizational issue, a team issue or an individual issue? Or was it just a bad idea, broken process or just bad timing? Get input from others inside and outside the team when analyzing a mistake.

☐ **6. Develop those who learn best.** If you are the team leader and you discover that you really do have one or more high-potential members on the team, learn how to manage them more effectively. They may not only contribute to the team and raise the performance bar for the other team members, but they may also be future executives in the making.

To change or develop a new skill, the person must:

- Have challenging, uncomfortable tasks/assignments. This was at least 70% of reported skill development in all firms. Essentially, development is doing the skill or failing at something important to you. All lousy listeners have had countless opportunities to learn. They don't because under stress they fall back on their strengths. Tasks that develop listening or anything else are those in which **not doing it is not a viable option**—coaching children's sports, running a task force of computer experts when you barely know how to turn one on, negotiating with someone who doesn't want to negotiate with you and doesn't really have to.

- Have continuing feedback on where he or she is on the skill vs. a target of success. This can take the form of a developmental partner, keeping a written summary of what's working and not working and having that reviewed periodically, or preferably a formal assessment. There are three types of these that work well: 1) Having the person take a standard questionnaire 3-6 months into their change project; 2) Having an agreed-upon list of people answer what they would like to have this person keep doing, start doing or stop doing in the developmental area 3-6 months into their change project; 3) 360° performance appraisal which combines 1 & 2. Typically, an agreed-upon list of people both formally rates the person on a set of questions/competency statements and provides narrative comments which are typed and presented anonymously. The results of this are usually tied to bonus/merit increases, although sometimes they are directly tied to one's performance rating/compensation. Research indicates that without this further feedback, even the best developmental plan usually fails miserably.

- Have some new/different things to do—typically these come from coursework/reading and account for no more than 10% of development. The lion's share is self-learning from tough tasks, and the learning from other people that comes from feedback. Many people can benefit from studying models of the behavior. This is a more direct way to learn than reading and easier for most people to assimilate.

■ In studies of development, those who are best at it are high learners: they tend to get out of their comfort zone, try many different ways to improve and actively search for ways to make sense out of their experiences.

■ In summary, development involves forcing ourselves out of our comfort zone: we either 1) Use related strengths to attack an area (the person isn't easy with others, but does have integrity and a good sense of humor he can use to get started); 2) Compensate for the weakness by job structuring, work systems, or surrounding the person with those who are good in an area and can also coach or teach the person; or 3) Attack the weakness directly. This last one is most productive as long as we focus on a few key areas. One and 2 are better methods for dealing with so-so areas or hopeless areas (e.g. the person isn't creative, and research shows this takes 10 years to develop even if the person has some latent capacity; better to let the person galvanize those who are creative, defer to others, or structure it out of the person's job).

More help? See FYI For Your Improvement™, Chapter 19—Developing Others. Read *The Leadership Machine* by Michael M. Lombardo and Robert W. Eichinger and *High Flyers: Developing the Next Generation of Leaders* by Morgan McCall.

☐ **7. Leverage GroupWare technology.** New communication and transportation technology have made new kinds of high-performing teams possible. Cheap, fast and easy communication makes it possible for some high-performing teams to function, even while members are physically distant from one another. In the new age of globalization in organizations, technology is one key factor in performance. Use e-mail, send faxes, schedule video conferences, and provide video cameras for employees who telecommute. Get creative with technology to bring team members together. While it doesn't take the place of being face-to-face, technology can play a role in building teams.

☐ **8. Get unstuck.** Is the team stuck in its ways of doing things or stale in its approach? If so, inject new information and approaches. Teams develop and learn when they get new and fresh facts or different perspectives on things that inside team members may not be able to provide. Look for ways to be resourceful and to gain new insight. Benchmark a competitor. Identify best practices outside the team. Bring in an outsider. Interview your customers. Learn the principles of total quality management or process reengineering. Read about the teams that win the Malcolm Baldrige Award or the *Business Week* Best Team competition. Study workflows around you. Then, make sure you find ways to use the new information. *More help? See FYI For Your Improvement™, Chapter 63— TQM/Reengineering.*

☐ **9. Contribute members to cross-functional teams.** Working on cross-functional teams or taskforces creates a unique opportunity for team learning. Viewing a problem or an opportunity from many angles can provide some exciting payoffs for an organization and for each team that has a member in the group. Look for ways to see possible changes on the horizon that may cause problems or provide opportunities for new products, systems or services. Bringing together people from a variety of disciplines with diverse backgrounds and thinking styles can increase the possibility for team learning.

☐ **10. Use change agents in the team.** Do some team members rock the boat so much that they make the rest of the crew seasick? Are these members free spirits who lack patience, discipline or due process courtesies in the process of their breakthrough discoveries? The challenge for the team leader and members is to find ways to integrate those differences within the team. Here are a few ways to keep the creative always forward-moving types creating, while at the same time keeping some level of peace and balance within the team:

■ Keep the creators challenged. You can do this by delegating or by empowering them to come up with their own assignments and workload. They don't like to be bored.

■ Recognize their contributions and give feedback when they aren't taking the needs of others into consideration. They want to know how they are perceived.

- Create a method of having them share their creative ideas with the rest of the team, especially those who think differently than they do.

- Don't overdirect creators or tell them how to get results, solve problems or make decisions. They like to figure it out on their own, and many times come up with improved team processes along the way.

SUGGESTED READINGS

Katzenbach, Jon R. and Douglas K.Smith, *The Wisdom of Teams*. New York: HarperCollins. 1993.

Lipman-Blumen, Jean and Harold J. Leavitt, *Hot Groups— Seeding Them, Feeding Them & Using Them to Ignite Your Organization*. New York: Oxford University Press, Inc. 1999.

Lombardo, Michael M and Robert W. Eichinger, *The Leadership Machine*. Minneapolis: Lominger Limited, Inc. 2001.

McCall, Morgan W. Jr., *High Flyers: Developing The Next Generation of Leaders*. Boston: Harvard Business School Press. 1997.

Parker, Glenn M., *Cross-Functional Teams*. San Francisco: Jossey-Bass, Inc. 1994.

TRANSLATION TO THE LEADERSHIP ARCHITECT® COMPETENCY LIBRARY

In order for a team or individuals on a team to perform well in this area, these are the competencies that would most likely be in play. Aside from a team improvement plan where everybody works on the same thing, some individual team members may need to work on some of these competencies. A critical number (but not necessarily all) of team members would have to be good at:

MISSION CRITICAL:

- ☐ 32. Learning on the Fly
- ☐ 33. Listening Skills
- ☐ 51. Problem Solving

IMPORTANT:

- ☐ 2. *Dealing with* Ambiguity
- ☐ 35. Managing and Measuring
- ☐ 45. Personal Learning
- ☐ 50. Priority Setting
- ☐ 62. Time Management

NICE TO HAVE:

- ☐ 28. Innovation Management
- ☐ 54. Self-Development
- ☐ 61. Technical Learning

In addition to the ten tips listed for this cluster, there are additional tips that may apply from *FYI For Your Improvement*™. Below are the four items from the TEAM ARCHITECT® that make up this cluster. The item number appears to the left of each item. Immediately below the text of each item are competency and tip numbers from *FYI*. The competency is listed first (from 1 to 67), followed by the tip number (1 to 10). For example, 33-4 refers to competency 33 (Listening), tip number 4. The tips are generally written for individual development so some adaptation might be needed in the team context.

10. The team debriefs its successes in order to find "repeatables" and perform better.

    15-10; 32-1,2,3; 33-4,5; 50-3; 51-1,3,8

28. The team debriefs its failures and mistakes in order to perform better.

    2-1,7; 29-5; 32-3; 33-7; 34-3,4; 35-2,7; 44-6

46. The team practices continuous improvement; team members are more skilled than they were a year ago.

    32-1,2,3; 35-2; 51-1,2; 53-1,3; 54-10; 63-6

64. Team members are receptive to innovative approaches and new technology to improve its effectiveness.

    14-2,8; 28-1,4,5,7; 32-2,3; 46-1; 61-7

11

TEAMING SKILLS—Operating the team's business efficiently and effectively

Decision Making—Did the team have trouble making key decisions in a timely way? Were the decisions the team made the right ones?

UNSKILLED

☐ Team spends too much time problem solving and collecting information at the expense of making timely decisions

☐ Team spends too much time getting everyone's input, approval or concurrence before making decisions

☐ Team members are too quick to decide; overuse their gut or don't seek out enough information

☐ Team endlessly debates decisions but stops just short of making them

☐ Team has internal cliques or alliances that dominate decision making

☐ Decisions are made off-line, outside of open decision making processes

☐ Some team members may use subjective approaches to decision making

☐ Team members cover their true feelings to keep peace, leading to less than timely and correct decisions

☐ Team churns the decision making process over and over with no end result

SKILLED (TEAM ARCHITECT® ITEMS WITH NUMBERS)

☐ (11) The team makes timely decisions; everything is not open for endless debate and fact finding

☐ (29) All decisions do not have to be made as a team; based on expertise, one or a few may make decisions at times

☐ (47) Team members resist jumping to conclusions

☐ (65) Team members discuss problems objectively; they do not form coalitions to pressure others into agreement

☐ Team uses different approaches to decision making, based on the situation

☐ Team has a process to follow when it needs to make complex decisions

☐ The team is comfortable making significant decisions before all the data is in

☐ Team is quick to correct a previous decision when additional information is known

☐ Team members rotate and step up to being decision managers

OVERUSED (TOO MUCH OF A GOOD THING)

☐ Team may make decisions too impulsively

☐ Team may make decisions too quickly to avoid debate and conflict on the issue

☐ Team may be too patient with the decision making process; the team tolerates unlimited debate

☐ Team may not collect enough information to make good decisions

☐ The team may leave others behind as it rockets through decisions

☐ The team may have trouble backing up and reprocessing a decision when additional information comes in

☐ Team may be so speedy that others with legitimate input are not given a chance

☐ Team may cause other teams to strain to keep up with collateral decision making

Note on overused strengths: Strengths used too much or too singly tend to have the negative effects listed above. To decrease those negative consequences, you have two alternatives. You can scale down or use the strength less or you can compensate for it with another skill or behavior. In practice, it is very difficult to get an individual or a team to use a strength less. Therefore, the best path is to develop compensators. Below are listed other TEAM ARCHITECT®

clusters that would compensate for overusing this dimension and compensating skills from the LEADERSHIP ARCHITECT® library of 67 competencies.

COMPENSATING TEAM CLUSTERS: 10, 12, 14, 20

COMPENSATING COMPETENCIES: 12, 17, 40, 41, 51

SOME CAUSES OF POOR PERFORMANCE

☐ Team does not handle uncertainty or ambiguity comfortably

☐ Team avoids the conflict involved in debating sides of a decision

☐ Some members need too much information to make a decision

☐ Team procrastinates; team is afraid to make a bad decision

☐ Team has had blowouts on previous decisions that have burned members

☐ Team has little perspective or a narrow outlook on issues

☐ Team members may be impatient

☐ Team may make timely decisions but they are not followed up on with the implementation plans they need

☐ A single key team member tends to hold things up

☐ A single key team member is extremely conservative

☐ A single key team member is not a clear-headed problem-solver

☐ The team starts a decision making process with answers and solutions before the issues have been properly defined

THE MAP

Decisions. Decisions. Making good decisions is easier than making timely decisions. Making timely decisions is one of the top developmental issues for teams. Most teams, given all the data and unlimited time, can make good and accurate decisions. The problem is with timely. Timely means before we're ready. Before we're comfortable. Before we have all the data. Before everyone on the team is on board. Before everyone feels they have had a fair shot at giving input. So timely almost always means in less time than we would want. Making decisions before we are ready increases the chance that the decision isn't exactly correct. It takes tolerance of ambiguity and uncertainty. It means not fearing mistakes. The second part of timely that is troublesome for teams is a timely making decision process. Too much debate and collaboration. Too much time between action points. Decisions lying in inboxes too long. Decisions waiting on someone who is not readily available. Decisions waiting for political clearance. Decisions waiting on information. Good decisions are based upon a mixture of data, analysis, intuition, wisdom, being patient enough to collect the available information, being humble enough to ask for other people's opinions and thoughts, and then coolly making the decision in time to be competitive. Teams must be able to identify the problems and opportunities they face, evaluate the options they have for moving forward, and then make the necessary trade-offs and decisions about how to proceed. Correct isn't enough. Correct enough in time to create competitive advantage is the key.

SOME REMEDIES

☐ **1. Overcome decision making challenges.** There are several challenges that must be met in order for an effective team decision to be made:

- **It must be timely.** Most teams have "windows of opportunity" that quickly open and shut. These could be driven by the organization's culture or politics, the impatience of the team sponsor or a pressing customer need, among other things. Decisions often need to be made, and action taken, very quickly.

- **It must be of acceptable quality.** You need to get decision making as right as possible the first time. There may not be a second chance. The competition is waiting for you to make a mistake. Therefore, decisions need to be on the mark and well thought out.

- **It must foster commitment in the team.** It won't do your team any good to make a fast and accurate decision if no one is going to listen, support or implement it.

- **It must foster commitment in others.** The customers of the decision must be satisfied with it.

More help? See FYI For Your Improvement™, Chapter 16— Timely Decision Making and Chapter 17—Decision Quality.

☐ **2. Make quality decisions.** In the pure light of day, making quality decisions is fairly easy and straightforward. You define the problem or issue that needs a decision. You collect all of the available information. You create multiple solutions. You check history for precedents and pitfalls. You test run those solutions and decisions to check their downstream positive and negative impact. You test the decisions with some other experts on this issue. You choose the one that has the best chance of success. You make the decision and move on. The only problem is that this takes time and discipline. When teams are studied making decisions, the major finding is that they do not take the up front time to define the issue. They start with solutions, conclusions, how they have done this in the past, and summary statements. So the first thing to have the team do is spend scheduled time defining the issue. No one is allowed to offer a solution. All that is allowed is to define aspects of the issue. The next step is to define the goal of the decision. What goal will be accomplished? What is being determined? How would it be measured? Then have the team create multiple solutions. Solution research shows that generally the first solution people generate is not the best one. Somewhere between the 2nd and 3rd solution is the highest quality solution. Then have the team spend a little time test-driving the decisions. Unintended consequences is an all too common problem. The decision causes some noise or negative consequences for others that were not anticipated. Once the solution is selected and the decision made, monitor what was intended with what actually happens and make course corrections as you go.

☐ **3. Pick the right people to make decisions.** It's hard enough to make an individual decision. It's harder for a team. Ideally, everyone has a piece of the puzzle. Everyone is without bias and contributes evenly. The discussions are balanced and the time managed efficiently. When the decision is made, the whole team is supportive and feels ownership because of involvement. In real life, contributions to a solution and a decision are unbalanced. Some have significant contributions to make and others have little to offer or even have a chilling effect on a correct decision. Teams need to be careful to not mix up the need for inclusion, collaboration, consensus and participation with

DECISION MAKING 11

109

making quality decisions. High-performing teams allow unbalanced inputs and distributed authority to those who have the best to offer, decision by decision. There is less need in a high-performing team for collaboration just for the sake of collaboration. Collaboration is used when more than one person has the pieces and parts needed to put together a good decision. Have the team decide for each decision that needs to be made who is the best person or combination of people to make the decision. Ask the team members who has information or strong preferences they would like to offer. Have the team internally delegate as much of the decision making as possible so the whole team doesn't have to take up its time working through decisions to which they do not add value.

☐ **4. Make timely decisions.** Most individuals and therefore, most teams have more trouble making timely decisions than accurate ones. This is usually due to the fear of mistakes and failures and the low tolerance for ambiguity and uncertainty. It also comes from the unrealistic expectation of perfection. Always making the right decision is the unfortunate standard. The important measure for individuals and teams is net accuracy over time. There are no perfect decisions in real life. All decisions turn out to be something less than perfect. Have the team discuss its expectations for accuracy and goodness of decisions. Compare that to other relevant teams. Timeliness is making a decision before you really are ready or want to. For most, making quick decisions is hard because it opens them up to potential criticism. Have the team set out a timetable for making timely decisions. Set an end date. Work backwards from there to lay out the decision making process. Along the way, periodically check with the team and poll them as to what they would decide if the decision were due in the next five minutes. Track that data over time to check to see when the team settled in to what turns out to be the final decision.

☐ **5. Make timely decisions in teams.** The complicating element when teams have to make timely decisions is the diversity of decision making style and preferences in the team. A few individuals are comfortable making seat of the pants decisions. More are comfortable taking more time and thinking things through. This inevitably leads to noise and conflict in teams as the slow paced resist the speed merchants. Try this approach. Do a team assessment, either self-ratings or, better yet, have the team members rate each other on comfort with making timely decisions. Line up the members of the team from speed-demons to reflectives. When the team anticipates having to make a significant decision, have the reflectives and the slower-paced work on it first, defining the elements and analyzing the issues. Have the three most conservative decision makers present their analysis to the three more comfortable with intuitive decision making. That way, they will all start from about the same place. The intuitives will be seeing the issue for the first time and the reflectives have had time to look at the issue in detail. While we wouldn't recommend you necessarily do this all the time, you should try different approaches to decision making. The "let's all get together and talk about it" approach rarely works. *More help? See Chapter 10—Team Learning, in this book.*

☐ **6. Learn how to make better decisions**—Individuals on teams need to have skills that are different from those needed in an organization built around individuals. Members need to be able to problem solve, make timely decisions, make quality decisions, and relate well to others in a team setting. These skills can make or break a team's ability to make fair and reasonable decisions, be open in their communications, confront one another, work through conflict and develop an effective approach to decision making. If too many members are lacking in these key skills, a team is likely to be inefficient. Consequently, teams will have unproductive meetings trying to get decisions made and work done. To improve team decision making ability, have individuals focus on their personal development and training around any gaps that may get in the way of them being a productive contributor on the team. The team should collectively participate in some team-building exercises to learn how to integrate the skills of individual members and develop decision making methods that make sense for the team and the business challenges. When quick decisions are needed, a team may need to delegate them to certain team members (who may be experts in the area) so they can be expedited. In other circumstances, it may be more appropriate for everyone to provide input and reach consensus. The way in which the team makes its decisions may vary, so in order to do that effectively, team members should be trained together so they can determine how the team will make decisions in certain situations and how they will deal with one another.

☐ **7. Use different decision methods.** Decision making doesn't come in one size. Teams need to be flexible in determining what type of decision making method is called for based on the business challenge at hand. Variety works best in teams. Too much decision making regulation can slow a team down. Make sure the team understands the different ways a decision can be made and uses the best approach for each situation. The important thing is that the team must decide in advance what decision making method will be used for the pending issue. No surprises in the decision making process midway. Here are some of the most common methods:

■ **Autocratic**—Made by one person (the team leader, sponsor, etc.) or a small group of individuals with expertise and the power. This method is useful for simple, routine, administrative decisions or when team members lack the skills or information to make the decision.

■ **Expert**—Some/one person or a few together are experts on this topic. This method is useful when the expertise of one person is so far superior to all other team members that little would be gained from team discussion.

■ **Democratic**—Everybody contributes, gets a vote and majority wins. This method can be used when there isn't time for consensus or when the decision is not so important that consensus is necessary. Be careful not to alienate those who didn't vote for the decision.

■ **Consensus**—A critical mass majority agree with the decision. Everyone may not agree, but the team has reached a point where everyone will support the decision. All team members agree to support the decision. This method is helpful in situations where you can take the time to hammer out a decision, but not practical in emergency situations or when there are extreme time pressures.

■ **Unanimous**—Everyone agrees that the best decision has been made. This method is useful when 100% member commitment is critical for implementing the decision.

☐ **8. Use time limits and summaries.** Is the team taking too long to make decisions? Are members rambling on and on and repeating themselves each time the debate gets heated? Studies show most decision making activity piles up in the last period before a deadline regardless of how long the group has had to work on the problem. Groups procrastinate just as individuals do. To speed up the decision, try to set a time limit for the discussion. Make the decision based on what you have talked about up to that point. Use a team coach or facilitator to keep track of decisions made during team meetings, so that a team can monitor the amount of work getting done when the team is together. Have the coach pull together the data already discussed and summarize it prior to each decision the team makes. It will help to get the team focused and ensure that all sides of the issue have been heard and considered.

☐ **9. Use decision managers.** A good technique is to use a decision manager. Studies have shown that the decision making process has a lot of downtime where nothing is being done. As much as 85% of the time the decision is laying in someone's in basket, on the bottom of the pile of things to do or in the briefcase in the car. If each decision has a manager, that person can walk the decision through the various input and approval steps needed to move the decision along. The decision manager also manages the discussions and debates over the decision. The decision manager makes sure everyone with input has a place to provide it. That all sides of the issues are examined. That expert advice is sought from outside the team. It's best if the decision manager is not involved passionately in the decision. This technique serves a dual purpose. Not only does it speed decisions, it offers development for decision managers on how to manage decision making processes.

☐ **10. Don't ask for input on a decision if you don't intend to use it.** This tip is especially for team leaders and decision managers. One of the best ways to kill trust in your team is to lead team members to think their opinion about the decision really affects the decision. Team members know when you are jerking them around. Don't ask if you aren't going to consider the input or if you have already made up your mind. If a decision requires you to use your authority without discussion, just say so.

SUGGESTED READINGS

Barner, Robert W., *Team Troubleshooter.* Palo Alto: Davies-Black Publishing. 2000.

Fisher, Kimball, Steven Rayner, William Belgard, and the Belgard-Fisher-Rayner Team. *Tips for Teams: A Ready Reference for Solving Common Team Problems.* New York: McGraw-Hill, Inc. 1995.

Katzenbach, Jon R. and Douglas K. Smith, *The Wisdom of Teams.* New York: HarperCollins. 1993.

Lawler, Edward E. III, *From the Ground Up.* San Francisco: Jossey-Bass, Inc. 1996.

Robbins, Harvey and Michael Finley, *The New Why Teams Don't Work—What Goes Wrong and How to Make it Right.* San Francisco: Berrett-Koehler Publishers, Inc. 2000.

TRANSLATION TO THE LEADERSHIP ARCHITECT® COMPETENCY LIBRARY

In order for a team or individuals on a team to perform well in this area, these are the competencies that would most likely be in play. Aside from a team improvement plan where everybody works on the same thing, some individual team members may need to work on some of these competencies. A critical number (but not necessarily all) of team members would have to be good at:

11

MISSION CRITICAL:

☐ 16. *Timely* Decision Making

☐ 17. Decision Quality

☐ 51. Problem Solving

IMPORTANT:

☐ 12. Conflict Management

☐ 33. Listening Skills

☐ 50. Priority Setting

☐ 53. *Drive for* Results

NICE TO HAVE:

☐ 1. Action Oriented

☐ 2. *Dealing with* Ambiguity

☐ 11. Composure

☐ 18. Delegation

☐ 42. Peer Relationships

In addition to the ten tips listed for this cluster, there are additional tips that may apply from *FYI For Your Improvement*™. Below are the four items from the TEAM ARCHITECT® that make up this cluster. The item number appears to the left of each item. Immediately below the text of each item are competency and tip numbers from *FYI*. The competency is listed first (from 1 to 67), followed by the tip number (1 to 10). For example, 33-4 refers to competency 33 (Listening), tip number 4. The tips are generally written for individual development so some adaptation might be needed in the team context.

11. The team makes timely decisions; everything is not open for endless debate and fact finding.

    1-5,7; 16-1,2,3,5,6,7; 50-9; 51-1

29. All decisions do not have to be made as a team; based on expertise, one or a few may make decisions at times.

    18-2,5,9; 53-2; 56-3,5; 60-3,8; 110-4,8

47. Team members resist jumping to conclusions.

    11-2,3,9; 33-3,6,7; 41-4,7; 51-1,2

65. Team members discuss problems objectively; they do not form coalitions to pressure others into agreement.

    12-1,2,4,7; 27-1; 34-8; 51-1,2; 57-2,4

12

TEAMING SKILLS—Operating the team's business efficiently and effectively

Conflict Resolution—Was there excessive noise and unresolved conflicts that took up time and kept people from working well with one another?

UNSKILLED

☐ Some team members avoid discussing uncomfortable subjects and let things fester for too long

☐ Conflict is seen as negative and avoided if at all possible

☐ Team members lash out at each other or shut members down in times of conflict; conflict gets personal

☐ Team members take too many conflicts to the team leader for resolution

☐ Conflict drives the team off course and disrupts normal processes

☐ The team's internal communications are ineffective and inconsistent

☐ The team has trouble building consensus when conflicts arise

☐ There is a lot of unnecessary noise in the team

☐ It takes too much time for the team to settle down and work together again after a particularly heated conflict

SKILLED (TEAM ARCHITECT® ITEMS WITH NUMBERS)

☐ (12) The team has smooth, freely flowing internal communications

☐ (30) The team takes on the tough issues; the ones many teams would rather not surface

☐ (48) The team can have an exciting contentious discussion and then reach a consensus

☐ (66) When a serious internal conflict occurs, the team calmly resolves it

☐ Team members listen to one another

☐ Team surfaces conflicts early

☐ All team members work to contain conflicts to the issues

☐ There are few surprises inside the team

☐ Those team members on the losing side of an issue don't brood, they become part of the loyal opposition and move on

☐ Surfacing and resolving conflict is seen as just a normal part of the team's business

OVERUSED (TOO MUCH OF A GOOD THING)

☐ Team is too quick to take on tough issues before they are allowed to settle on their own

☐ Team spends too much time opening and discussing conflicts

☐ Team tries too hard to resolve the unresolvable

☐ Some team members cave in to consensus just to smooth over conflict

☐ Team members may be too accommodating and over anxious to keep peace in the team

☐ The team's internal conflicts may spill out to others around them and be misinterpreted as more negative than they are

☐ It may be really hard for a new member to be comfortable due to the open atmosphere and immediate airing of everything

☐ Team may get buried in communications and emails they don't need to know or even want to know

Note on overused strengths: Strengths used too much or too singly tend to have the negative effects listed above. To decrease those negative consequences, you have two alternatives. You can scale down or use the strength less or you can compensate for it with another skill or behavior. In practice, it is very difficult to get an individual or a team to use a strength less. Therefore, the best path is to develop compensators. Below are listed other TEAM ARCHITECT® clusters that would compensate for overusing this dimension and compensating skills from the LEADERSHIP ARCHITECT® library of 67 competencies.

COMPENSATING TEAM CLUSTERS: 1, 9, 11, 14, 15, 20

COMPENSATING COMPETENCIES: 2, 41, 48, 51

SOME CAUSES OF POOR PERFORMANCE

- ☐ Members just want to get along and be liked
- ☐ Some members avoid conflict at all costs
- ☐ Team leader doesn't set a good example on handling conflict
- ☐ Organization is conflict adverse; conflict is viewed as politically incorrect and negative
- ☐ Members are shy and reluctant to surface issues
- ☐ Members may take conflict too personally or are too sensitive
- ☐ Team turns little things into conflicts because they enjoy the battle
- ☐ Members are uneven in terms of their tolerance and skills at handling conflict
- ☐ Team views all conflicts as either winning or losing

THE MAP

There is good news and bad news. The good news is that conflict can be the elixir to better solutions and more effective problem solving. Conflict brings out differences of fact and opinion and experience. It adds heat to the fire. It brings things from under the table to the light of day. It puts passion behind the debate. All can put forth their views. All can play. In the end, if it were a fair and open process, the issues and challenges would be better met. Conflict can lead to better and more lasting solutions because all sides are heard and nothing is held back. The bad news is that the majority of people are reluctant to face open conflict. Conflict is chilling rather than energizing. Conflict is uncomfortable rather than motivating. Conflict hurts and is personal more than constructive or a means to an end. Conflict decreases personal effectiveness rather than being a means to peak performance. In a team, just one or a couple of individuals can be conflict averse and hold the rest of the team back. For those who are comfortable with conflict, it is a lifelong blessing in all areas of life. For those who are conflict averse, it is a dead weight affecting team performance as well as not getting top service in a restaurant because they will not send back a bad meal.

SOME REMEDIES

☐ **1. Accept that conflict is normal and necessary.**
Just like trust, conflict is a necessary part of becoming a high-performing team. Rarely can you expect a group of people to come together, build a common purpose, set performance goals and measures, assign roles, produce results and not run into some significant conflict. Key to getting through this necessary evil is to make conflict constructive and not something that must be painfully endured or tolerated by team members. Teams learn through conflict and become stronger, just as individuals learn through personal hardships. The most effective team members intercede when other team members are in conflict, to help resolve the disagreement proactively. Bad or weak team members turn their backs on conflict and either ignore it and hope it will disappear or let the other team members battle it out. Don't let the good guys always get stuck resolving the conflict. Find opportunities to debrief conflict at team meetings to make sure members don't miss the meaning from the experience, and/or fall into the same traps over and over.

☐ **2. Identify the causes of conflicts.** One or a combination of the following reasons generally causes conflicts. Teams need to recognize the causes of their conflicts to effectively work on them and prevent recurrences. Usually the identification of causes is the first step to resolving a conflict successfully.

- Unmet individual needs and wants
- Clashing values
- Different perceptions
- Varying knowledge
- Different assumptions
- Different expectations
- Different backgrounds

■ Willingness and ability to deal with conflict

Review the list of causes with the team and discuss examples for each cause. Identify constructive ways to resolve the examples discussed. Post the list of causes somewhere that is visible to team members. Refer to the list of causes when conflicts arise to facilitate understanding and resolution of disagreements within the team.

☐ **3. Identify the cost of conflict.** Conflict can go beyond being just an irritant for team members. It can be expensive. As a result, teams should look at unresolved conflict as affecting the bottom line, justifying the need for it to be actively managed. If conflict avoidance or ineffective conflict resolution becomes a regular challenge, consider trying to identify the cost of conflict. Have each team member privately identify a team conflict that they have either participated in or observed. Ask the team members to individually identify the costs associated with the conflict that came to mind using this criteria or other criteria that best suits the team:

■ Delayed decisions

■ Wasted time

■ Reduced or poor decision quality

■ Turnover or terminations

■ Loss of resources

■ Restructuring/restaffing to accommodate the conflict

■ Sabotage/damaged reputations

■ Lowered motivation, reduced performance and productivity

■ Absenteeism associated with the conflict

■ Stress related health costs

Ask for a show of hands to gauge the total range of costs associated with the conflict that each team member assessed, i.e., less than $100, $100-$1,000, $1,000-$10,000, etc.

Mention that these were cost examples of just one conflict. Imagine what the collective conflicts add up to. Discuss the implications of each category used in the analysis. Identify ways to reduce costs associated with conflict in the future.

☐ **4. It's just business: Tackle the issues, not the people.**
It's likely for teams to have a tendency to avoid negative or uncomfortable subjects. Some team members may even be sensitive to initiating tough discussions because they don't want to be perceived as "rocking the boat." Lingering conflict that is not surfaced will eventually block performance and productivity. Get over your fears. Some members may also avoid conflict because they are afraid they won't be able to enlist support from others in the group to their position. They don't want to lose. They avoid situations where people need to side with one camp or the other. Generally speaking, teams shouldn't need to get themselves into situations where conflict gets overly personal. A way to overcome some of these fears is to help teams learn how to focus conflict resolution more on things and issues and less or not at all on people. Most conflicts have to do with process anyway, the "what," not the "who." Collective focus on the process or the team goals will bring people back together to work toward improving performance. It should also lessen common defensive behaviors that can surface in times of conflict. Make statements that focus on the issues, not on John or Sally. The simplest choices of words can temper discussions and allow the team to focus on resolution rather than getting sidetracked on personal attacks that will leave hurt feelings and scars that might take time to heal, if they ever do. *More help? See FYI For Your Improvement™, Chapter 12— Conflict Management.*

☐ **5. Practice civilized disagreements.** When teams work closely together they are bound to have disagreements from time to time and perhaps a less than harmonious existence. When it seems like the team (or someone) is about to blow, team members should work to create a climate that supports civilized disagreements. The book *Leading Self-Directed Work Teams: A Guide to Developing New Team Leadership Skills*, by Kimball Fisher notes the following tips:

- **Stay focused on the task/issue**—Look past the interpersonal styles and biases to maintain an objective, logical approach to the conflict between team members.

- **Be flexible**—There has to be some give-and-take on both sides; high-performing teams require all members

122

to be able to adjust their actions based on the needs of each situation.

■ **Lighten up**—A little humor can cut the tension and diffuse a heated situation before it blows. Just remember to laugh with, not at a team member.

■ **Back off**—It takes two to tango. Is your position being rejected by the group? If so, don't force the issue if it isn't going anywhere. Read your audience. Try a new approach. Take a break from the situation. Consider that maybe you might be wrong.

More help? See FYI For Your Improvement™, Chapter 2— Dealing with Ambiguity, Chapter 26—Humor, and Chapter 45—Personal Learning.

☐ **6. Re-establish team conflict rules of engagement.** If there are one or more persons on a team who are causing trouble by not behaving constructively during times of conflict, you should consider revisiting team norms or rules of engagement to deal with them as a group. The team leader (or team coach/facilitator) should facilitate a discussion of team member expectations about how conflict is to be handled in the team. Develop a list of norms or acceptable behaviors. These should be things like listening to opposing views, letting each person be heard, staying objective, no interrupting, no shouting, voting if consensus cannot be reached, etc. Team conflict norms have two functions: 1) They provide a guide for self-monitoring by team members, and 2) They provide a basis for the team leader or member to give feedback to another member who has violated a norm. Use the discussion on developing a set of conflict norms to lead to an assessment of how well the norms are currently being followed. Assuming everyone wants the team to succeed, most problems center around a lack of communication and the absence of a method for complete discussion of tough issues.

☐ **7. Anticipate organizational or political conflict traps.** High-performing teams learn how to deal with conflict through frank and open communication. That, however, is easier said than done. Many people grow up in large companies where they are taught to play by the rules of politics. Conforming to politics can usually contribute to

12

career success. Lack of it is sure to derail people at some point. Learning to speak within accepted boundaries is generally key to becoming a political success. The conditioned responses that are learned emphasize respecting your superiors, supporting the party line and not pushing crazy or overly creative ideas in a conservative culture, to name a few. These political responses generally include restricting conflict and making it difficult and risky to surface conflict. If your organization is extremely political, create new rules within the team to get past it. Make a commitment to keep confidences about things that may be taboo in the rest of the organization. What happens in the team stays in the team. Successful teams find ways to open up to conflict and respond constructively to one another. This allows individual differences to be surfaced, understood, and ultimately merged into common goals. *More help? See FYI For Your Improvement™, Chapter 48—Political Savvy.*

☐ **8. Build consensus.** Consensus is different than consent. Consent usually means majority rule. Consensus is a decision everyone can live with and generally involves compromise among teammates. All team members must agree, even though their preferred solution may not be the one the team is ultimately going with. However, they do see the agreed-upon solution as acceptable, having a mindset of "I can live with the decision." The key to consensus is give-and-take within the team. Offering ideas, respecting differences and taking in other viewpoints by listening to the opinions of your team members are critical behaviors. It is a lot easier to do this if there are previously established norms and beliefs that everyone's facts, opinions and even feelings matter. When facilitating a consensus decision, leverage the following tips:

- Focus on the idea or solution, not by whom or how it is being suggested

- Look for a "meet me half way" option most people can live with

- Analyze the reality of the idea having success in the team, organization or marketplace

- Analyze the cost-effectiveness of the option

Decisions made via consensus take more time and should be seen as win/win propositions, rather than winning and losing camps within the team on the issue.

☐ **9. Discuss the undiscussables.** Undiscussables are those things everybody knows are issues on the team, but they are rarely discussed openly as a group. The more silent, the more deadly they can be. Teams are inversely successful to the number of issues that remain under the table. The more undiscussables there are, the less successful the team. Undiscussables are sticky issues, like the team leader who isn't up to standard, a team member that takes all the credit, a team member that isn't carrying his or her load, or the team numbers that get fudged at the end of the month to make it look like the team is hitting their goals. Undiscussables are generally kept under the table. They need to be carefully surfaced. Utilize a coach or facilitator to help put the undiscussables atop the table. Give each team member three index cards to write down three separate undiscussable issues. The facilitator should collect them and briefly review to see if there are any trends. A code of conduct or rules of engagement should be established to make the exchange productive. The facilitator should post the first most common undiscussable and ask questions to prompt discussion:

- What does this undiscussable mean?
- What is the cause?
- What is the cost?
- What prompts this issue if it reoccurs?

If the team agrees that it is something that needs to be fixed, or assign an action item to, the facilitator might ask these types of questions:

- What are barriers to overcoming this undiscussable?
- What resources do we need to fix it (sponsorship, money, time, etc.)?
- What are the consequences of not fixing it?
- Who will own this?
- How will we measure progress?

125

☐ **10. Other conflict tools and concepts:**

■ **Use a conflict manager or facilitator or coach.**
Sometimes it is difficult for a team to solve its own
conflict problems. The team is too close to the problem. It
might be helpful to bring in a facilitator or conflict coach
from time-to-time for an outside perspective. An outsider
can sometimes say what members inside the team can't
or won't. Bringing in an outsider is not a sign of
weakness, just a realistic view of how difficult conflict is to
harness for some teams.

■ **The loyal opposition.** Even the best of teams don't
reach complete consensus on everything. There are
always individual team members who are not happy with
the result of the resolution. But in high-performing teams,
they join the loyal opposition on that issue. What this
means is that they will present and support the decisions
or resolution of the team publicly. The team knows they
disagree and the rest of the members respect that.
The disagreements are kept inside the team. There is no
off-line processing or politicking to get the decision
changed. There is no talking outside school—"the team
decided X but I still believe Y is the right answer."

■ **Make time for conflict.** Conflict takes time but the
results are generally worth it. Anticipate those topics that
are conflict loaded and give them more time on the
agenda. Be careful to not cut off debate until all sides are
heard. If an issue is too hot to resolve, carry it over to the
next meeting.

■ **Name an issue manager.** It's best if the issue manager is
not part of the debate. The issue manager is the
timekeeper, the rule enforcer, and the synthesizer. The
issue manager decides who gets to talk and for how long.
The issue manager keeps the debate focused on the
issues and away from personalities.

■ **Everything can't be win-win.** Sometimes team
members will feel passionately about an issue, but the
consensus will go against them. At these times, it is
critical to support them immediately after the decision
because they may be feeling alienated or even stupid that
the issue didn't go their way. Generally, all that is needed

is some acknowledgment that losing is no fun, that we all lose some, and that they are valued contributors.

SUGGESTED READINGS

Argyris, Chris, *Strategy Change and Defensive Routines*. Boston: Pitman. 1985.

Barner, Robert W., *Team Troubleshooter*. Palo Alto: Davies-Black Publishing. 2000.

DeBono, Edward, *Six Thinking Hats*. Toronto: Key Porter Books. 1985.

Fisher, Kimball, *Leading Self-Directed Work Teams: A Guide To Developing New Team Leadership Skills*. New York: McGraw-Hill Professional Publishing. 1999.

Katzenbach, Jon R. and Douglas K. Smith, *The Wisdom of Teams*. New York: HarperCollins. 1993.

Parker, Glenn M., *The Handbook of Best Practices for Teams, Volume I*. Amherst: HRD Press. Burr Ridge: Irwin Professional Publishing. 1996.

Robbins, Harvey and Michael Finley, *The New Why Teams Don't Work: What Goes Wrong and How to Make it Right*. San Francisco: Berrett-Koehler Publishers, Inc. 2000.

TRANSLATION TO THE LEADERSHIP ARCHITECT® COMPETENCY LIBRARY

In order for a team or individuals on a team to perform well in this area, these are the competencies that would most likely be in play. Aside from a team improvement plan where everybody works on the same thing, some individual team members may need to work on some of these competencies. A critical number (but not necessarily all) of team members would have to be good at:

MISSION CRITICAL:

☐ 11. Composure
☐ 12. Conflict Management
☐ 34. Managerial Courage
☐ 42. Peer Relations

IMPORTANT:

☐ 27. Informing

☐ 33. Listening

☐ 51. Problem Solving

NICE TO HAVE:

☐ 37. Negotiating

☐ 50. Priority Setting

☐ 57. Standing Alone

In addition to the ten tips listed for this cluster, there are additional tips that may apply from *FYI For Your Improvement™*. Below are the four items from the TEAM ARCHITECT® that make up this cluster. The item number appears to the left of each item. Immediately below the text of each item are competency and tip numbers from *FYI*. The competency is listed first (from 1 to 67), followed by the tip number (1 to 10). For example, 33-4 refers to competency 33 (Listening), tip number 4. The tips are generally written for individual development so some adaptation might be needed in the team context.

12. The team has smooth, freely flowing internal communications.

    27-2,3,4,10; 33-3,4,5; 42-1,7; 105-1

30. The team takes on the tough issues; the ones many teams would rather not surface.

    12-3,4,5,7; 34-3,9; 43-1,5; 57-1,4

48. The team can have an exciting, contentious discussion and then reach a consensus.

    12-1,3,4,5,7; 17-3; 34-3; 51-1,2,3

66. When a serious internal conflict occurs, the team calmly resolves it.

    11-3,9; 12-2,3,4,5,7; 41-7; 51-1,2

13

TEAMING SKILLS—Operating the team's business efficiently and effectively

Team Atmosphere—Was the atmosphere inside the team conducive to everyone performing at their best?

UNSKILLED

- ☐ The tone in this team is chilling and negative
- ☐ Individuals look forward to the time they are no longer part of this team
- ☐ Team members show little or no connectivity to one another; they have little in common
- ☐ Team doesn't take the time to celebrate or recognize performance milestones
- ☐ Some team members are all work and no play
- ☐ Individuals on this team would not pick one another as friends or colleagues in the open market
- ☐ The team does not spend any off work time together
- ☐ The team has cliques that tend to do things together but not with others
- ☐ Openings on this team are hard to fill; people with talent are reluctant to join the team
- ☐ This team's lack of a positive atmosphere spills over and affects others above and below them
- ☐ There isn't much if any team pride, just individual pride or satisfaction

SKILLED (TEAM ARCHITECT® ITEMS WITH NUMBERS)

- ☐ (13) The team has an identity; it is not just a collection of individuals
- ☐ (31) Team members enjoy working on this team

- ☐ (49) The team has a positive atmosphere that is commented on by those outside the team
- ☐ (67) The whole team celebrates its successes
- ☐ High-performing/high-potential employees want to work on this team
- ☐ Openings on this team are easy to fill
- ☐ Team members have a true concern for others on the team, even beyond work
- ☐ Team members truly enjoy one another as people
- ☐ Team not only works hard together, they also play well together
- ☐ Others who report to members of this team comment on how well they work together and how positive the tone is

OVERUSED (TOO MUCH OF A GOOD THING)

- ☐ Team is too consumed with itself and one another
- ☐ Team members may have too much fun, spend too much time socializing and bonding
- ☐ Team is perceived as too tight a clique
- ☐ Team celebrates so much that others perceive them as arrogant
- ☐ It's extremely difficult for a new team member to fit in because the team is so close
- ☐ Team spends too much effort trying to outdo other teams
- ☐ Team is so close that it is hard for outsiders to gain access
- ☐ Team spends so much time with one another that they do not build effective networks outside the team
- ☐ Sometimes members are reluctant to get negative for fear of chilling the positive atmosphere

Note on overused strengths: Strengths used too much or too singly tend to have the negative effects listed above. To decrease those negative consequences, you have two alternatives. You can scale down or use the strength less or you can compensate for it with another skill or behavior. In practice, it is very difficult to get an individual or a team to use a strength less. Therefore, the best path is to develop compensators. Below are listed other TEAM ARCHITECT® clusters that would compensate for overusing this dimension and compensating skills from the LEADERSHIP ARCHITECT® library of 67 competencies.

COMPENSATING TEAM CLUSTERS: 1, 9, 12, 15, 18, 20

COMPENSATING COMPETENCIES: 3, 21, 42, 53, 65

SOME CAUSES OF POOR PERFORMANCE

☐ Team members may not have had enough time to bond

☐ Team leader may not create an atmosphere that encourages fun or celebration

☐ Organization is overly formal or stiff and doesn't promote fun at work

☐ Team members can't relax or loosen up

☐ One or more team members are negative and spoil all the fun for the rest

☐ There is a lack of humor in the team

☐ Team is made up of apples and oranges with little in common

☐ Team is under great stress and time pressure and has little time for anything else

☐ The way the team is organized and the work is distributed does not really require cooperation and/or much interaction

THE MAP

Aside from family and a person's religion, work takes up a very large and significant portion of life. And aside from the physical rewards of money and incentives, people look for psychic income from their work. They want a boss who is positive. Positive in the sense of someone who they respect, and perhaps like, who treats them as a person and listens to them. They also want to work in an environment that's positive and energizing. They want to work for a winner. They want to have pride in their work. Almost anyone would prefer to be on a high-performing work team than one that trails the pack. They also want to enjoy what they do, work with people they enjoy and work in an environment they enjoy. Although people have a view of what enjoyment is, generally it's having some amount of fun doing what they do. It's a positive can-do tone. It's an environment of mutual respect and trust. It's people they can relax with. It's a team that supports its members. People like to belong. They especially like to belong to a team that wins and enjoys it along the way. And of course the research says these are two of the requirements for being a high-performing team.

SOME REMEDIES

☐ **1. Do atmosphere audits.** In the everyday workplace, everyone is busy and there is not much time to stop and reflect. Everybody is hunkered down and doing their work. Even so, it's important that the atmosphere of the team be periodically monitored. The monitoring can range from the very simple asking one-on-one or in team meetings how things are going, to more formal surveys of morale. The drivers of a positive atmosphere are factors like trust in the leader and coworkers, fairness in assignments and evaluation, energy around doing something worthwhile, and just reward for accomplishments. It's also important to surface atmosphere-chilling issues sooner rather than later. A team can quickly lose its positive feel when things go wrong. Here you are looking for noise and barriers. The question would be, "What's keeping you from performing and having fun doing it?" Other tips about what to look for can be found in *Love 'Em or Lose 'Em* by Beverly Kaye and Sharon Jordan-Evans.

☐ **2. Plan off work activities**. Allow for time for members of the team to get to know one another outside work. All work and no play don't make for the most effective team environment. Some off work activities are especially important in the early stages of team development. Sometimes they happen naturally, because a member invited the team to happy hour on Friday afternoon and they all end up spending a little social time together. Other times they are scheduled events. If you are the team leader and your team hasn't had any off work activities, schedule something. Some events should be team members only and others should include significant others and families. Invite the team over to your house for a cookout. If your company sponsors different community events, get tickets to a sports event or concert to bring the team together. These gatherings will allow people to see team members from new perspectives and appreciate their differences, and ultimately understand them more clearly. They also help to create a bond of common happenings and pleasant experiences.

☐ **3. Celebrate successes.** When is the last time the team had a party? If the team hasn't had a party lately, maybe there hasn't been a formal excuse to celebrate. Effective teams find things to celebrate about. Celebrations keep energy levels high in the team. Find accomplishments and outcomes that warrant a celebration. Order pizza. Bring in a cake. Give everyone a shirt or something to recognize the team achievement. Look for ways to lift morale through celebration.

☐ **4. Help new team members get onboard.** One of the most challenging tasks a team can face is the introduction of a new member. New team members and leaders are added all the time to already formed teams. Teams can't get too comfortable with the way things used to be once there is a new member. This may cause some sacrifice and temporarily slow down the performance of the team. However, the team needs to roll their sleeves back up and spend some time re-forming. Otherwise, the new team member won't get a fair start and will most likely struggle adapting into the new environment. The team should create an orientation process for the new member. Here are some ideas of things to include to help ensure the success of the new member:

- Team charter and goals. Check for clarity to make sure the new team member understands the purpose of the group. Given the fresh perspective, does the team member have any value-adding suggestions?

- Role clarity for the new member. Map out his or her role and explain the roles of other members.

- A candid assessment of how the team is doing. What's working, what isn't, what's needed.

- Team supplier, customer, and competitor data.

- Team values and rules of engagement. It is a good idea to revisit and amend to include the new team member. You can't just expect him or her to have the same values initially.

- Organizational boundaries and guidelines the team follows. Political or cultural issues.

- Miscellaneous group processes (regular meeting times, presentations, workflow, etc.).

- Skills or competencies needed for success on the team.

- Training to learn needed technical or functional skills.

- Use lunch times and coffee breaks for socialization to get to know the new member personally.

- If the team has a favorite social spot, restaurant or place where they celebrate, take the new member there early on as part of their initiation process.

- Ensure the new member has the appropriate necessities: phone, computer, e-mail, desk, security access, etc.

- Give the new member a significant assignment from the start that will expose her or him to key constituencies.

Finally, while everyone on the team should have a part in the orientation of the new member, it may help to assign the new team member to a buddy who will be responsible for ensuring that the orientation is actually completed. Make this person accountable for the new team member's on-boarding process. Rather than holding back until the rest of the team is sure the person is the right fit, assume fit until events prove otherwise. Trust first.

☐ **5. Work on the team's sense of humor.** Teamwork can be stressful. Teamwork can be intense. Teams can be given short-term, high-impact, heavy-workload assignments that force them to spend more time with each other than they do with their own families. Humor can make or break tense situations like this. Think about a person you know with the least amount of humor. Imagine working 10 hours a day with that person 5 days a week. Now think about someone with a great sense of humor (also assuming this is a productive person). Wouldn't it be a lot more tolerable to be confined to a workspace with the humorous person? Members need to learn how to laugh at themselves and laugh with (not at) their teammates. Use humor and discussions of non-work subjects to relieve tension and smooth over awkward moments. Post funny cartoons and articles, joke about yourself (that's usually safe), or point out the lighter side of events. *More help? See FYI For Your Improvement™, Chapter 26—Humor.*

☐ **6. Use mistakes and failures as learning opportunities.** Mistakes happen. The key is to learn from them and to create an atmosphere that is free of fear around mistakes. If the team leader or team members make others feel bad about mistakes, risk taking will become stifled, mistakes will be hidden and blaming will dominate. And learning will decrease. Teams can use mistakes as learning opportunities. Here are some suggestions to make it happen:

■ The team leader and team members should talk about mistakes openly without embarrassment around the team.

■ Team members should respond constructively and maintain composure with a teammate who has made a mistake.

■ Keep feedback on the mistake focused on the process or problem at hand, rather than on personalities, etc., unless the team member's behavior was the issue.

■ Create strategies to immediately recover with the business, sponsors or customers when mistakes are made.

■ Have a regular team meeting agenda item on learning from mistakes so that others can learn from things that have happened.

■ Present an award to the team member whose resolution of a mistake created the most learning for the team.

☐ **7. Allow work time for banter, rapport building and small talk.** Team effectiveness can be enhanced when the people on the team really respect each other and get along. It's a good sign when team members are talking and laughing with one another, as long as the environment stays productive. Tolerate seemingly unproductive chatter throughout the day. Save time before, during or after meetings for members to socialize or just catch up on things in general that may be company related or personal. Some teams develop their rituals to make this happen on their own. A training team in a large insurance company once set up a long meeting table just outside their row of cubicles. The team used to hold regular weekly meetings at this table so

135

they could remain close to their workspace. Then the table evolved into the morning place to bond. Every morning between 8:00 and 8:30 a.m. the team members would arrive with their cup of coffee and chat about the training they delivered the day before, new customer requests, what they watched on TV the previous evening, and anything else that came to mind. It was a positive way to start each day. It was the way they stayed connected and developed relationships that lasted beyond the life of the team's charter. The team referred to its space as the "kitchen table" to symbolize the sense of home and family that they felt.

☐ **8. Energy and enthusiasm.** Effective teams work hard and enthusiastically. They also play hard and enthusiastically. This energy and enthusiasm creates an environment for performance. When energy is high, people are motivated to succeed. You don't have to ask members to put in extra time, they just do it. They hit targets with minimal direction. They find creative ways to knock down barriers. Outsiders and onlookers can observe the energy. They can also feel it when they enter the team's space. The energy attracts others to join the team. The energy cannot be mandated or prescribed by the leader or the organization. It just happens. And it happens primarily from the interactions of the team members. If your team is lacking this energy, use a facilitator or coach to help determine why things seem flat. Consider getting feedback from outsiders to learn about their perceptions of the team. The feedback can help to pinpoint or at least surface some issues that might be dragging down the team.

☐ **9. Have more fun.** Research noted in *The Wisdom of Teams* by Jon R. Katzenbach and Douglas K. Smith found there were several common threads among high-performance teams. One such thread is that high-performance teams have fun. The fun is a by-product of the team's sense of commitment to each other and performance. If your team doesn't seem to be having fun, consider examining the cause and effect learned from this research. Are the team members committed to the goals of the team? *If not, see Chapter 3—Thrust Commitment, in this book.* Are the team members committed to one another? *If not, see Chapter 6, Trust Inside the Team.* Fixing one or both of these issues might result in more fun.

☐ **10. Win.** Long-term team enjoyment is more due to being on a winning team than most anything else. Nothing fixes morale problems faster than consistently meeting and exceeding your goals. So time spent on goal alignment, talent deployment, process and outcome measurement, and the adroit use of the team's resources will all add positively to the atmosphere in the team. Setting priorities and aligning the work to be done with the interests of each team member goes a long way in solving atmosphere issues. So basically, try to work your way out of a negative atmosphere and then be sure to celebrate the wins.

SUGGESTED READINGS

Fisher, Kimball, Steven Rayner, William Belgard, and the Belgard-Fisher-Rayner Team. *Tips for Teams: A Ready Reference for Solving Common Team Problems.* New York: McGraw-Hill, Inc. 1995.

Katzenbach, Jon R. and Douglas K. Smith, *The Wisdom of Teams.* New York: HarperCollins. 1993.

Kaye, Beverly and Sharon Jordan-Evans, *Love 'Em or Lose 'Em.* San Francisco: Berrett-Koehler Publishers, Inc. 1999.

Parker, Glenn M., *Team Players and Teamwork.* San Francisco: Jossey-Bass, Inc. 1996.

Robbins, Harvey and Michael Finley, *The New Why Teams Don't Work: What Goes Wrong and How to Make it Right.* San Francisco: Berrett-Koehler Publishers, Inc. 2000.

TRANSLATION TO THE LEADERSHIP ARCHITECT® COMPETENCY LIBRARY

In order for a team or individuals on a team to perform well in this area, these are the competencies that would most likely be in play. Aside from a team improvement plan where everybody works on the same thing, some individual team members may need to work on some of these competencies. A critical number (but not necessarily all) of team members would have to be good at:

TEAM ATMOSPHERE

13

MISSION CRITICAL:

- ☐ 36. Motivating Others
- ☐ 60. *Building Effective* Teams

IMPORTANT:

- ☐ 26. Humor
- ☐ 27. Informing
- ☐ 42. Peer Relations
- ☐ 53. *Drive for* Results

NICE TO HAVE:

- ☐ 29. Integrity and Trust
- ☐ 65. *Managing* Vision and Purpose

In addition to the ten tips listed for this cluster, there are additional tips that may apply from *FYI For Your Improvement*™. Below are the four items from the TEAM ARCHITECT® that make up this cluster. The item number appears to the left of each item. Immediately below the text of each item are competency and tip numbers from *FYI*. The competency is listed first (from 1 to 67), followed by the tip number (1 to 10). For example, 33-4 refers to competency 33 (Listening), tip number 4. The tips are generally written for individual development so some adaptation might be needed in the team context.

13. The team has an identity; it is not just a collection of individuals.

    60-1,3,6,7,8; 36-3,10; 110-1,2,4

31. Team members enjoy working on this team.

    27-2,3; 60-1,3,6,7,8; 36-3,10; 110-4

49. The team has a positive atmosphere that is commented on by those outside the team.

    36-3,10; 42-2,5,6; 53-6; 60-1,3,4,7

67. The whole team celebrates its successes.

    36-3,10; 60-1,3,7; 110-1,2,8,9

14

*TEAMING SKILLS—Operating the team's business efficiently
and effectively*

**Managing Process—Were the processes the team used to do
its work efficient and effective?**

UNSKILLED

☐ Team members utilize haphazard or unsystematic work
processes without developing clear methods or best practices

☐ Team seldom does things right the first time, even though
they may fix it eventually

☐ Team has a "not invented here" mentality and does not seek
out best practices

☐ Team members do not anticipate problems or roadblocks

☐ Team members let process problems fester for too long

☐ Team members blame one another, the team leader or the
organization for not hitting performance targets

☐ The team does not accept responsibility for
performance breakdowns

☐ The team does not fix performance breakdowns in a
timely fashion

☐ Team has had trouble implementing TQM/Process
Reengineering/ISO or similar workflow systems in the past

SKILLED (TEAM ARCHITECT® ITEMS WITH NUMBERS)

☐ (14) The team spots problems early and works to
eliminate them

☐ (32) The team makes no excuses for not meeting performance
goals; it identifies and attacks the causes of missing the mark
and fixes them

MANAGING PROCESS 14

139

- ☐ (50) The team is process-driven; it is relentless in streamlining workflows
- ☐ (68) The team is excellent at designing new processes that work well the first time
- ☐ The team develops best practices that are leveraged by others
- ☐ The team readily scouts for and uses best practices from others
- ☐ The team is always tinkering with processes and reengineering for optimal performance
- ☐ The team places a high value on efficient and effective processes and workflows
- ☐ The team has measurement systems that provide early warnings on broken processes
- ☐ The team is more problem solving than blame-focused when things don't go right

OVERUSED (TOO MUCH OF A GOOD THING)

- ☐ The team's emphasis on single best methods chills innovation and creativity
- ☐ The team attempts to correct workflow problems too quickly before really assessing true damage
- ☐ The team spends too much time looking for problems
- ☐ The team may be too hard on itself when performance goals are missed
- ☐ Team members may be overly critical of one another and leave scars that are difficult to repair
- ☐ Team spends too much time perfecting processes at the expense of net productivity
- ☐ There is so much pressure on performing that the joy is gone
- ☐ It is extremely hard for a new team member to fit in because everything is so specified and certain

Note on overused strengths: Strengths used too much or too singly tend to have the negative effects listed above. To decrease those negative consequences, you have two alternatives. You can scale down or use the strength less or you can compensate for it with another skill or behavior. In practice, it is very difficult to get an individual or a team to use a strength less. Therefore, the best path is to develop compensators. Below are listed other TEAM ARCHITECT® clusters that would compensate for overusing this dimension and compensating skills from the LEADERSHIP ARCHITECT® library of 67 competencies.

COMPENSATING TEAM CLUSTERS: 1, 2, 9, 18

COMPENSATING COMPETENCIES: 7, 28, 36, 50, 51

SOME CAUSES OF POOR PERFORMANCE

☐ Team members avoid the conflict of challenging processes and workflows

☐ Team members may not be process-oriented; not systems-oriented

☐ Organization may not value best practices or TQM/Process Reengineering/ISO

☐ Members may be resistant to input from outside the team

☐ Team has high turnover; takes too long to orient new members

☐ Team may be arrogant

☐ Team members may be impatient with process design

☐ Things don't stay the same long enough for results to be measured

THE MAP

There are research based and experience tested systems and processes for designing workflows and processes. They go under a number of names. Total Quality Management. Process Reengineering. ISO. Process Engineering. Industrial Engineering. Time and Motion Studies. Most of these processes start with the end in mind, usually the customer, and design the process backwards with the least number of steps and the fewest resources per unit or service produced as possible. The methods also include a measurement element so the team can monitor results, and a continuous improvement component that constantly looks for opportunities for improvement. In most workflow processes that have existed for a few years or so, there are wasted steps and excess resources. Most workflow processes have 15%

PROCESS

14

MANAGING

to 35% excess time, steps, and resources in them when these methods are not applied. In many studies of unexamined workflow, there is 85% downtime when the work is just suspended between steps or people. You can't have a high-performing work team without effective and efficient processes. That takes some discipline and technology. The technology is readily available.

SOME REMEDIES

☐ **1. Study workflow technologies.** Have members of the team explore the various workflow technologies. There are many to choose from. Many varieties of TQM. Process Reengineering (Hammer and Champy). Six Sigma (GE is a good example). ISO (mainly in Europe). Plus more. The objective would be to see which of those various methods might best fit the work of the team. Have each member study a technique and report to the team on his or her findings. Have the team decide which method best fits the needs of the team. Many organizations already use one or more of these techniques. Check with others in the organization to see if there is already a group that uses any of the techniques. Invite them in to present what they are doing.

☐ **2. Do a study of workflow efficiency and effectiveness.** Using one or more of the techniques identified above, do a study of the workflows used by the team. Lay out each process step-by-step to see if each step is really needed and how much each step costs in terms of resources. Starting from the customer, design each process with as few steps and with the least resources possible. Look for unnecessary signatures. Unnecessary reviews. Products and services stuck in inboxes of an out of the office member. Look for where the most errors occur. How can they be prevented? Unnecessary features the customer didn't ask for. Unneeded permissions. Blocked access to resources. Learn how to use workflow software and apply it to the critical processes the team uses to perform.

☐ **3. Hire a process expert or consultant to help.** Sometimes it is best to leave things to the experts. There are many process methods available in the market. If your team is under time pressures, inexperienced with process or if the project has high stakes, consider hiring a process consultant or consulting organization that specializes in your industry. Check references to ensure customer satisfaction. Find out who will be your lead consultant and supporting consultants. Engage the consulting firm to "transfer the technology" to the team. This means to not only analyze the processes but to teach the team how to do it on their own in the future.

☐ **4. Recognize common process breakdowns.** Look for trends where high-frequency and high-impact problems occur with the processes. *Measuring Team Performance* by Steven D. Jones and Donald J. Schilling identifies the following common breakdowns in processes:

- Duplicate steps or work
- Unnecessary, non-value adding steps
- Excessively time-consuming activities
- Manual work that might be easily automated
- Overly complex steps
- Steps that could be combined
- Steps or activities in the wrong order
- Lack of compliance with certain steps
- Steps frequently resulting in waste or rework
- Steps that result in user or customer complaints
- Missing steps that are typically added by performers

Once the team has identified one or more breakdowns, determine adjustments that need to be made in response. Not all processes need to be reengineered; instead, they may just need tweaking. Others may only require clarification. Maybe people haven't been informed about how the process works. Or, maybe they have not fully understood communications and training regarding the process.

☐ **5. Create a series of process and outcome measures.** Process measures ensure that disconnects and breakdowns do not creep back into the process. The measures must be developed to reflect either the extent to which the process produces the desired outputs, the degree to which certain steps have been performed, or both. Here are some key steps to follow when creating process measures:

- Identify subprocesses or activities within the team that are most closely linked to the team's primary products and services. This should be the work most crucial to meeting customer and business results.

- Narrow the work to measure (in Step #1) down to the most critical processes. These should be processes that add the most value to the customer and advance the business.

- Quantify the outputs of the processes.

- Flowchart the processes and subprocesses to help identify the steps or activities worthy of measurement.

☐ **6. Make process measures open and visible.** Ever notice how athletes keep their eye on the clock and the scoreboard? They're checking their progress against time, the competition and ultimately, winning the game. Use signs or technology to post team goals, processes, data and progress toward accomplishment. It's the idea behind the United Way thermometer. It's the number of days without a work-time injury. This constant reminder will help to clarify understanding, keep the organization involved and motivate performance.

☐ **7. Have regular performance/goal review meetings.** The team must make certain the processes are monitored and continually improved. Make this a standard team meeting agenda item. Enlist regular feedback efforts or surveys to determine if processes are really meeting customer and business requirements. The team should determine if the process is meeting its objectives as well. After gathering data, the team should initiate corrective actions to move the feedback into developmental and improvement strategies.

☐ **8. Leverage new workflow monitoring technology.** Organizations should carefully consider work and organization design when they choose technology to use with their processes for things like manufacturing or service work. Many teams and companies make the mistake of thinking technology first and workflow or process second. Don't separate work design from technology. When technology is chosen in advance or as a stand-alone effort, it can have a limiting effect on workflow options.

☐ **9. Assign team members to search for best practices outside the team.** On a regular basis, have team members scout and scan for best practices outside the team. Have each member report back what they find and have the team decide whether it should adopt the new or improved practice.

☐ **10. Do roadblock scenario planning.** On a periodic basis, have the team take one process at a time and do a roadblock analysis. The task is to envision what all could go wrong. Play out various scenarios where there are breakdowns in the processes the team uses to produce its products and services. Look for substandard quality. Misplaced orders. Misunderstood specifications from the customer. Delivery errors. Badly handled customer services inquiries. Typos in instructions. Missing parts. Errant invoices. Payments not logged properly. By thinking about all of the things that could go wrong, the team can design-in checks and balances so all of the bad things won't happen.

SUGGESTED READINGS

Jones, Steven D. and Don J. Schilling, *Measuring Team Performance: A Step-by-Step, Customizable Approach for Managers, Facilitators, and Team Leaders.* San Francisco: Jossey-Bass, Inc. 2000.

Lawler, Edward E. III., *From the Ground Up.* San Francisco: Jossey-Bass, Inc. 1996.

TRANSLATION TO THE LEADERSHIP ARCHITECT® COMPETENCY LIBRARY

In order for a team or individuals on a team to perform well in this area, these are the competencies that would most likely be in play. Aside from a team improvement plan where everybody works on the same thing, some individual team members may need to work on some of these competencies. A critical number (but not necessarily all) of team members would have to be good at:

MISSION CRITICAL:

☐ 51. Problem Solving

☐ 52. Process Management

IMPORTANT:

- ☐ 53. Drive for Results
- ☐ 63. TQM/Reengineering

NICE TO HAVE:

- ☐ 1. Action Oriented
- ☐ 16. *Timely* Decision Making
- ☐ 32. Learning on the Fly
- ☐ 47. Planning
- ☐ 50. Priority Setting

In addition to the ten tips listed for this cluster, there are additional tips that may apply from *FYI For Your Improvement*™. Below are the four items from the TEAM ARCHITECT® that make up this cluster. The item number appears to the left of each item. Immediately below the text of each item are competency and tip numbers from *FYI*. The competency is listed first (from 1 to 67), followed by the tip number (1 to 10). For example, 33-4 refers to competency 33 (Listening), tip number 4. The tips are generally written for individual development so some adaptation might be needed in the team context.

14. The team spots problems early and works to eliminate them.

    16-2,3; 32-2,3; 51-1,3; 52-3,6,8; 63-1

32. The team makes no excuses for not meeting performance goals; it identifies and attacks the causes of missing the mark and fixes them.

    16-2,3; 32-2,3; 43-1; 51-1,8; 52-3,8; 53-3

50. The team is process-driven; it is relentless in streamlining workflows.

    51-1,3; 52-3,4,6,8; 63-1,2,3,6

68. The team is excellent at designing new processes that work well the first time.

    51-1,3; 52-3,4,6,8; 62-1,2,3,6

15

TASK SKILLS—The effort necessary to get the job done

Focusing—Did the team have trouble setting and following priorities?

UNSKILLED

- ☐ The team may try to focus on too many things at once
- ☐ The team doesn't focus enough attention on the customer
- ☐ The team has too much of an inward focus
- ☐ Team members are too tactical
- ☐ The team misses goals and targets
- ☐ The team may have hit-and-miss approaches to priority setting
- ☐ Team members may spend too much time on less or unimportant things
- ☐ Team members may be easily distracted and prefer working on fun/exciting things at the expense of staying focused on the critical few
- ☐ The team struggles when priorities shift
- ☐ The team is surprised by changing trends and shifts in customer requirements

SKILLED (TEAM ARCHITECT® ITEMS WITH NUMBERS)

- ☐ (15) The team focuses more on its customers than on itself
- ☐ (33) The team's strategies are insightful and successful
- ☐ (51) The team's tactics and annual plans are on target
- ☐ (69) The team focuses on the critical few priorities; it is not easily diverted
- ☐ The team easily shifts focus as things change
- ☐ The team has measurements in place that track progress against priorities

☐ The team is constantly on the prowl for changes and trends that will affect its priorities

☐ Team members are in personal and constant touch with customers

☐ Each major action the team takes is first tested against its priorities

OVERUSED (TOO MUCH OF A GOOD THING)

☐ Team may be overly responsive to customer needs, sacrificing internal practices and policies

☐ Team members may be workaholics

☐ Team may respond to unreasonable customer requests and lose focus

☐ Team may oversimplify plans

☐ Team may be impatient with day-to-day, tactical details

☐ Team may become too rigid with their priorities and not be flexible enough to meet changing customer or organizational needs

☐ Limiting the priorities to too few may chill innovation and creativity

☐ Team may shift priorities too quickly on false signs of change

☐ Team may get out ahead of its customers before the anticipated need becomes viable in the marketplace

Note on overused strengths: Strengths used too much or too singly tend to have the negative effects listed above. To decrease those negative consequences, you have two alternatives. You can scale down or use the strength less or you can compensate for it with another skill or behavior. In practice, it is very difficult to get an individual or a team to use a strength less. Therefore, the best path is to develop compensators. Below are listed other TEAM ARCHITECT® clusters that would compensate for overusing this dimension and compensating skills from the LEADERSHIP ARCHITECT® library of 67 competencies.

COMPENSATING TEAM CLUSTERS: 1, 2, 10, 14, 18

COMPENSATING COMPETENCIES: 2, 9, 12, 28, 41, 53, 58, 65

SOME CAUSES OF POOR PERFORMANCE

- [ ] Team members may be undisciplined and disorganized
- [ ] Team members may not manage time well
- [ ] Team doesn't plan
- [ ] Team doesn't manage and measure work
- [ ] Team has one or more lagging performers
- [ ] Team members get easily diverted
- [ ] Individual team members do not agree with the priorities
- [ ] Team isn't customer focused
- [ ] Team may not interact enough with their customers
- [ ] Team members are impatient and impulsive and just react as things happen

THE MAP

Finite resources facing infinite demands. Most individuals, teams and organizations face more demands on their time and skills than they have to give. The key is to separate the mission critical few from the more trivial many. This process would be fairly simple were it not for two issues. The first is saying no. Picking a few critical priorities means turning down or delaying others. Each rejected priority has one or more customers. We have found that teams do not have a problem rank ordering priorities as much as saying no to those customers of the ones not selected. The second issue is that not all priorities are equally fun, exciting, "what I live for" or rewarding for everyone. The critical few priorities may not be highly motivating to individual team members. They may not be the ones the team wants to work on. There is not a successful manager alive that would not include in his or her commencement speech, "You have to focus your efforts on the mission critical few." Do not get distracted. Match resources with what you can and must deliver. If you are lucky enough to have time and resources left, start on the next most critical priority.

SOME REMEDIES

☐ **1. Align the team's efforts with the strategy/vision/goals.**
In some cases a team resides in an organization that has a clear vision, mission, a set of strategies and measurable goals. In that case, the process is one of alignment to achieve the appropriate team focus. The steps are:

- Get a clear understanding of the organization-wide vision, mission, strategies and goals. Invite someone from the organization who is familiar with them to come and present to the team. Encourage the team to ask lots of clarifying questions. Ask about the assumptions that were used to create the vision. Ask about the risks and unknowns. Ask about any future scenarios that may affect the vision. Ask what the organization expects from this specific team.

- In a team meeting, ask for suggestions about what parts of the organization-wide vision, mission, strategies and goals this team can add value to and support. Whether it's increased market penetration, better cost management, opening new territories or being the leader in customer service, most teams will find pieces and parts of the organization-wide thrust they can be part of.

- With as much specificity as possible, have the team outline the specific subgoals and tactics that support the organization thrust.

- Put all of the goals and tactics together into one plan to see if it works, given the resources of the team.

- Set measures ahead of time that will help the team track its performance against those goals.

- Present the plan back to the person or function that presented the organization thrust to find out if they see the plan as aligned and on target.

- Make any adjustments that might be necessary and execute the plan.

- Put all of this into a rank ordered set of priorities. What is mission critical and what's nice to have? What needs to be done first?

☐ **2. Meet periodically to reassess priorities.** The team's priorities will likely change. This could occur as a result of the larger organization changing its strategy or structure, customer requirements shifting, marketplace trends, or even a change in team membership and leadership. Teams must be flexible to maneuver accordingly. The team should keep its priorities and goals posted so team members see them every day. Use team meetings to review the work priorities of the group and of each individual. Help team members prioritize the efforts they have on their plates by keeping all good ideas on the list, but moving them up or down so the team can focus on its top priorities.

☐ **3. Start with the customer first and do a value chain analysis.** An independent or another way to set priorities is called a value chain analysis. The process starts with what the customer wants, needs, will pay for, or has requested. Then the planning process is backwards. In order to get customers what they want, we would need to be able to do …? In order to do that, we would need to be able to …? And so on. Then each step is resourced. What resources are needed to accomplish the right process outcomes for each step? Then who is going to be responsible for making sure that step is accomplished in sequence, on time, and at or under budget?

☐ **4. Install a trend and change scanning process.** Priorities shift. Things change. Customers change their minds. Teams need to anticipate and plan for change. Teams can lose time and waste resources during change. Put a member of the team in charge of tracking and speculating about change in:

- The organization surrounding the team
- The customers of the team, both internal and external
- Competitors
- Resources

Have each member report periodically to the rest of the team, suggesting the most likely changes. Have the team play out the change in terms of what the team would need to do to adjust.

☐ **5. Have a single point of contact with customers.** A team's success can sometimes be influenced by how well it interacts with (or pleases) its customers. Some teams

15

FOCUSING

designate specific team members as the client liaison, responsible for ongoing contact with customers. Having a single point of contact with customers is both efficient and effective because:

- It makes it easier for clients to give feedback.

- It allows the team to designate, train, and develop one person skilled in client interface.

- It eliminates undue confusion that occurs when too many team members talk to clients.

☐ **6. Get feedback from customers.** If the team is going to succeed, everyone on the team must really understand customer requirements. If the team wants their members to demonstrate extraordinary service, individuals should be skilled in handling difficult situations, be able to probe to identify customer needs and expectations, and go beyond the call of duty to provide exceptional service. If you want to find out what customers want, you need to ask them.

- **Direct contact with customers**—Having direct contact with customers can be very informative for team members, especially if the organization is in the type of business where most employees may not normally have routine customer contact. Have team members ask customers how the team is doing as the provider of a product or service? Ask detailed questions such as: What do we do best? What could we do better? What would you like to see us do differently?

- **Survey your customers.** Most companies survey their employees annually. Why not survey your customers too? The point is to gather more detailed data on key customer requirements. These include things like quality, accuracy, timeliness, value, comparison to the competition and likelihood to become a repeat customer. Gather this data and communicate the findings to the organization so resources can be aligned to respond to the customer feedback.

☐ **7. Plan the work and then work the plan.** It's easy for teams to get diverted into crisis management mode, things that are more fun, unnecessary diversions, or losing sight of the plan. There are really two parts to this puzzle. The first is to create a plan that, if executed, would accomplish the objectives. The second is executing the plan. Executing the plan is a matter of plan visibility and understandability. Do members of the team really understand the plan? Try to reduce the plan to individual work plans so each member has a clear template of what he or she needs to do. Throughout the year, keep referring back to the plan for guidance.

☐ **8. Put in measurements to track progress against plan.** The discipline of goals and measures co-exists with the reality of change. Recent research has shown that truly legendary leaders have two opposing sounding traits. One is the discipline of executing strongly against a well-thought-out plan and the other is being adaptable and open to change. This paradox—discipline and adaptability—probably extends to legendary teams. The world is changing faster than most of us are comfortable with. Success means having a plan, sticking to it, and executing the plan efficiently and effectively. At the same time, the team needs to be on the lookout for signs of change that affect the purpose and goals of the team. You can play this paradox two ways:

- When you set the plan, extend the discussion to include what the team would do if things change. Do a change analysis, listing likely change inside the team, to the organization in which the team resides, to the customers of the team and to the world outside the organization. Do change scenario planning to pre-determine how the team would change if anticipated change occurs.

- You can wait until something changes. The team would need a scanning discipline to detect internal or external change. When the early signs of change are detected, assemble the team of the affected individuals, and modify and adjust the plan.

The other way to think about this paradox is that a good plan will have an element in it that lays out the process for adapting to change midway down the road.

☐ **9. Stay on track.** It is easy for teams to get excited about their goals. Enthusiastic and high-energy teams sometimes have a tendency to jump into too many things at once. This can result in the team spinning its wheels, missing goals, frustrating members and lowering productivity. If the team

15

F O C U S I N G

starts to get off track consider some of the following tips:

- Pace yourselves by making sure team members aren't eagerly doing things before they should.

- Are all of the activities supporting the team plan and goals? If not, is the plan still valid? Or are the activities underway not the most important things for the team to be working on. Ask these questions to redirect efforts.

- Maintain an eye on process. Is the team working faster and better when it repeats processes?

- Is the team keeping a sense of humor? If not, are team members becoming overly aggressive or ambitious with their efforts? Is their behavior creating a toxic team atmosphere? *If the fun is gone or stifled by some team members, see Chapter 13—Team Atmosphere, in this book.*

☐ **10. Watch out for too much focus on work.** Sometimes there is a fine line between a passion for work and an obsession with it. Too much focus on work and team can put the rest of life out of whack. If one or more members of the team seem significantly out of balance and spending too much time at work, analyze the cause. Is the team understaffed? Are the objectives unrealistic? Are some members not carrying their fair share of the load? Are we inefficient and long hours are required? Work with the team leader to identify possible solutions and intervene with team members who are crossing the line.

SUGGESTED READINGS

Jones, Steven D. and Don J. Schilling, *Measuring Team Performance: A Step-by-Step, Customizable Approach for Managers, Facilitators, and Team Leaders.* San Francisco: Jossey-Bass, Inc. 2000.

Katzenbach, Jon R. and Douglas K. Smith, *The Wisdom of Teams.* New York: HarperCollins. 1993.

Lawler, Edward E. III, *From the Ground Up.* San Francisco: Jossey-Bass, Inc. 1996.

Parker, Glenn M., *Cross-Functional Teams.* San Francisco: Jossey-Bass, Inc. 1994.

Zook, Chris and James Allen, *Profit From the Core: Growth Strategy in an Era of Turbulence*. Boston: Harvard Business School Press. 2001.

TRANSLATION TO THE LEADERSHIP ARCHITECT® COMPETENCY LIBRARY

In order for a team or individuals on a team to perform well in this area, these are the competencies that would most likely be in play. Aside from a team improvement plan where everybody works on the same thing, some individual team members may need to work on some of these competencies. A critical number (but not necessarily all) of team members would have to be good at:

MISSION CRITICAL:

- [ ] 15. Customer Focus
- [ ] 50. Priority Setting

IMPORTANT:

- [ ] 5. Business Acumen
- [ ] 46. Perspective
- [ ] 47. Planning
- [ ] 53. *Drive for* Results

NICE TO HAVE:

- [ ] 35. Managing and Measuring Work
- [ ] 58. Strategic Agility
- [ ] 65. *Managing* Vision and Purpose

In addition to the ten tips listed for this cluster, there are additional tips that may apply from *FYI For Your Improvement*™. Below are the four items from the TEAM ARCHITECT® that make up this cluster. The item number appears to the left of each item. Immediately below the text of each item are competency and tip numbers from *FYI*. The competency is listed first (from 1 to 67), followed by the tip number (1 to 10). For example, 33-4 refers to competency 33 (Listening), tip number 4. The tips are generally written for individual development so some adaptation might be needed in the team context.

15. The team focuses more on its customers than on itself.

    15-1,3,4,5,8,9; 46-1; 53-1; 63-1,6

33. The team's strategies are insightful and successful.

    2-1,5; 5-6; 15-3; 46-3,9; 58-3; 65-10; 101-2,6

51. The team's tactics and annual plans are on target.

    5-6; 15-1,4; 16-2,3; 46-3; 47-1,3,7; 50-3

69. The team focuses on the critical few priorities; it is not easily diverted.

    16-3; 35-1,7; 43-1,2; 50-2,3,6; 53-3,4

15

16

TASK SKILLS—The effort necessary to get the job done

Assignment Flexibility—Did team members pitch in and help others get their work done?

UNSKILLED

- ☐ Team rigidly assigns certain work to certain members
- ☐ Some team members carry greater workloads than others
- ☐ Team does not give members developmental assignments outside their area of expertise
- ☐ Team members do not accept more than their assigned workload
- ☐ Team members do not help each other
- ☐ Team members do not cross-train to cover one another
- ☐ Team members are too specialized for cross-training to be practical
- ☐ Team members are micromanaged
- ☐ Each team member acts pretty much alone
- ☐ Each team member stays so busy that there is no time left for anything else
- ☐ Jobs are designed too narrowly

SKILLED (TEAM ARCHITECT® ITEMS WITH NUMBERS)

- ☐ (16) The team assigns work flexibly to team members
- ☐ (34) Team members pitch in and share the load
- ☐ (52) Team members have the autonomy needed to do their work
- ☐ (70) The team uses cross-training so team members can fill in for one another
- ☐ Roles are clear in the team

- [ ] Team members show interest in what other team members are doing
- [ ] Team members volunteer their help before they have to be asked
- [ ] The team sets aside time for learning from others inside the team
- [ ] Jobs are designed so that everybody does a little bit of everything

OVERUSED (TOO MUCH OF A GOOD THING)

- [ ] Team is too loose in the way it distributes work
- [ ] Team members are jacks-of-all-trades and masters of none
- [ ] Team members spend so much time helping one another that they don't get their individual assignments completed
- [ ] Team carries one or more lagging performers whose work is done by others
- [ ] It's hard for people outside the team to know who to go to on an issue
- [ ] Team has trouble focusing on the critical few tasks it needs to do
- [ ] Team members get used to variety and have trouble settling back into just their jobs
- [ ] Team members spend too much time looking for new things to learn and do
- [ ] New team members may have difficulty getting used to the extent of assignment flexibility
- [ ] Team members have trouble when they move on to other teams with less internal flexibility

Note on overused strengths: Strengths used too much or too singly tend to have the negative effects listed above. To decrease those negative consequences, you have two alternatives. You can scale down or use the strength less or you can compensate for it with another skill or behavior. In practice, it is very difficult to get an individual or a team to use a strength less. Therefore, the best path is to develop compensators. Below are listed other TEAM ARCHITECT® clusters that would compensate for overusing this dimension and compensating skills from the LEADERSHIP ARCHITECT® library of 67 competencies.

COMPENSATING TEAM CLUSTERS: 8, 14, 15, 18, 20

COMPENSATING COMPETENCIES: 13, 39, 50, 53

SOME CAUSES OF POOR PERFORMANCE

- ☐ The work of the team doesn't lend itself to cross-training; the work is too specialized
- ☐ Some team members have a fear of failing when they work outside their area of specialty
- ☐ Some team members can't deal with the ambiguity of flexible work assignments
- ☐ Team prefers structure
- ☐ Team is rigid
- ☐ Team leader is poor at delegating
- ☐ Some team members act like martyrs, doing everyone's work for them
- ☐ Some team members may overdo work/life balance
- ☐ Some team members may be workaholics
- ☐ Team is not made up of learners
- ☐ Team members prefer to work on their own
- ☐ Team members are comfortable in their specialties

THE MAP

A winning response to times of change is flexibility. Hardly anyone or any team is immune to the rapid change we are all experiencing. The team has tremendous demands coupled with a finite capacity to output work and services. An effective tool to deal with this problem is assignment and workload sharing and balance. With the exception of highly specialized teams or teams where each job is unique, all other teams have some degree of assignment flexibility. Some of that flexibility is in load balancing. It's almost always the case that one or a few team members are swamped and others are less busy. So elementary flexibility is that the less busy temporarily help the swamped until the crisis is over. Hopefully, when the tides shift, the helped will reciprocate and help the helpers. Morale and enthusiasm in load-balanced teams is generally higher than in teams where a few do all the work. More fundamental is task sharing where one member takes over a complete task either for learning and development or because that member is already better at that task. There is also task sharing for motivation, variety and building team strengths. Last, there is mission critical focus, where the team needs to put all of its resources into a very focused task that is a do-or-die for the team. So regardless of what job or role you play in the team, all hands are assigned and do well enough to fulfill the mission. Whether to deal with today's challenges or to prepare for an uncertain tomorrow, flexibility always wins over rigidity.

SOME REMEDIES

☐ **1. Do an analysis of what portion of each job might be general enough to be shared by others on the team.** Most jobs have general and specific parts to them—parts only a person with specialized skills can do and then more general parts that most anyone close to that job might do. Line up all of the jobs. List the 10 main duties or tasks that make up each job. List the 10 in order from the most specialized to the most general. Have other team members review the tasks and put their names next to the ones they think they could do. This sets up a basic system for load sharing and work balancing. You can also assign multiple people to each job: One as prime, the other as backup based upon what each member of the team puts down.

☐ **2. Design jobs so that task sharing is more possible.** In the extreme, jobs can be designed so that only people with very specialized skills can do them or they can be designed where the tasks are more evenly balanced across the team. The easier path is to put all of one type of task together and hire a specialist to do that. The bigger challenge is to design jobs so that each job has a little bit of everything in it. You could think of this as vertical or horizontal job design. Obviously, horizontal job design would lead to easier sharing and load balancing. One other benefit of horizontal job design is that you can bring generalists into the team, people who are skilled in the general area of the team's business but who are not specialists. In practice, there are more generalists available than specialists.

☐ **3. Ask each team member what parts of other people's jobs they might like to learn and do.** If previous cross-training efforts have failed, consider determining whether training requests/needs are based on skill deficiencies (people don't know how) or will deficiencies (people don't want to) before you decide to invest more time and money in training. If budgets and resources are tight, remind team members that cross-training is costly, is a time hog and creates a loss in initial productivity. Team members may be more motivated to learn if they've had some input on what they are going to learn and who they are going to learn it from. Therefore, solicit input from team members on the jobs or tasks they are interested in learning. A few things to consider:

■ Don't let people get cross-trained on jobs they aren't qualified for. These could be health, safety, technical or educational qualifications, among other things.

■ Determine if the technical requirements create too steep of a learning curve, thereby taking too long for an employee to get up-to-speed to be successful.

■ Allow people to make mistakes; create a learning environment.

■ Determine which jobs may only require one technical expert on the team, thereby eliminating the need to cross-train.

■ Be mindful of the time it takes to cross-train.

■ Recognize that people learn differently.

■ Don't allow people to cross-train on too many things at once.

☐ **4. Set up a reward system for helping others.** Rewards can be tied to specific objectives and they can also be spontaneous. A good reward system allows this flexibility. People like to be rewarded differently based on what motivates them: time off, a parking place, a memo from an executive or recognition from peers, etc. The rewards used in teams should encourage and reward behavior that is consistent with its overall strategy. Helping each other to achieve goals is certainly behavior that should be valued in teams. Some teams might have a rotating trophy or symbol that has special meaning to the team that they pass around for helping each other. Whatever it is, don't let the help go unnoticed. Celebrate teamwork and togetherness when it is displayed at its finest. It will create pride and a sense of spirit within the team.

☐ **5. Develop the performance capability of others.** What happens if a member on the team is struggling with performance? Does it frustrate other team members? How do they respond? Do they complain about that person to the other team members? Do they go to the boss? Do they shun that person because of it? If other team members recognize the performance gap and see the path to recovery, why aren't they helping that person discover it? Do they want the other member to fail? If not, members should take the lead to bring the person along. Developing others is generally the worst rated competency in managers. Developing others takes time more than anything. Use the opportunity to improve someone else's performance to help members on the team grow a skill that most don't have. *More help? See Chapter 10—Team Learning, in this book, and in FYI For Your Improvement™, Chapter 19—Developing Others.*

☐ **6. Set aside time to cross-train sensibly.** The days of single function, single task jobs are just about gone. Instead, most people who work in teams are now required to learn a variety of roles to support their team's daily activities. Cross-training provides several benefits:

■ It allows for more seamless service to customers, without the hassle of being transferred or passed off to a number of people to answer questions or get results.

■ It allows for cost efficiencies for the organization. Since cross-training eliminates many process steps and hand-offs, it can increase productivity and sometimes decrease the number of employees needed to provide a service or complete a task.

■ It provides increased job satisfaction. Employees are more fulfilled when they are doing a complete task and getting out of the rut of doing repetitive piecework.

Cross-training sensibly requires the team to plan, assess and implement.

- **Plan**—Identify and plan for the skills that will be important for team members to be successful. Involve all team members in this process. Identify the time requirements that will be involved for the cross-training so that productivity and service do not slip. Enlist other resources to help cover the time when the team may be cross-training.

- **Assess**—Assess each team member against the skills noted as important for the cross-training efforts. Identify the largest skill gaps. Prioritize the most critical skills and people to be trained.

- **Implement**—Cross-training requires discipline. It also requires time. Too often, we make excuses to not develop ourselves. We're too busy, other things are more important. Focus efforts on implementation and measure results. Make the time. No excuses.

☐ **7. Roll up your sleeves and pitch in.** Ever heard the saying there is no "I" in team? It can mean a number of things. It especially means letting go of individualism as it relates to taking credit for accomplishments and looking at work as anything less than a collective effort. Group and team effort means that your work isn't done until everyone's work is done. Good team members monitor their own work as well as those around them. They offer to help when they see a team member overloaded or when a team member has a more pressing priority than their own. Team members shouldn't have to be told to help out others on the team. It should come naturally from their commitment to the team goals and their commitment to one another. *More help? See Chapter 3—Thrust Commitment and Chapter 6—Trust Inside the Team, in this book.*

☐ **8. Get comfortable with ambiguity.** Role flexibility, assignment flexibility, cross-training and all the other elements of this topic have to do with change. Uncertainty requires flexibility. Flexibility requires comfort with ambiguity. Lack of ability to deal with ambiguity can be painful for individuals and paralyzing for a team. Nobody wants to play "52 pick-up" every day of the week, but the reality is that some days you'll go to work and have to do things that were not planned for or that you are not skilled for. The ambiguity

ASSIGNMENT FLEXIBILITY

16

of learning different roles and acquiring new skills presents team members with a challenge. If the challenge feels too great, practice unfamiliarity outside the team environment. Go to restaurants you've never been to before. Shop at a different grocery store. Vacation in places where you've done little research. *More help? See FYI For Your Improvement™, Chapter 2—Dealing with Ambiguity.* Or, team members can increase their individual and collective abilities to deal with ambiguity using the AMBIGUITY ARCHITECT®. Have individuals self-assess and combine their individual profiles to create a team profile. Look for skills and gaps that the team has collectively to raise the awareness of strengths and also the types of situations and change events that could be potentially problematic for the team. Create strategies for individuals to test their comfort with ambiguity, using job assignments to help them deal with turbulence.

☐ **9. Use vacations as an opportunity for cross-training.** Nothing forces a team member to rise to the occasion more than a challenge. If the team hasn't taken the time to cross-train individuals proactively, they'll have to do it to cover when a team member is out. A planned vacation or a prolonged trip might prove to be a great opportunity to make this happen. The vacationing or traveling employee should spend some time with the team member to be trained prior to his or her vacation or trip. Where possible, create a desk manual or some written documentation of key process steps to serve as a reference guide. Notify key constituencies ahead of time that there will be a different person to deal with for a brief period of time. Debrief the experience when the vacationing employee returns and hand over any work or assignments that were left undone while the person was away.

☐ **10. Set up a load mechanism so that it is visible to all when one member needs temporary help.** It's almost always the case that one or a few team members are swamped and others are less busy. Load-balancing is that the less busy temporarily help the swamped until the crisis is over. Hopefully, when the tides shift, the helped this time will reciprocate and help the helpers. Morale and enthusiasm in load-balanced teams is generally higher than in teams where a few do all the work. Set up a system for load-balancing. Have the team determine what the standards are and how the team is going to signal for help. Such a system is necessary because without standards, some will ask too often and others not at all. You have to set up a system where asking is shameless and blameless and help is freely given and rewarded. You might also set up standards for calling for outside help when the members of the team just can't be diverted to help. The system should be well understood by everyone to decrease or hopefully eliminate any "noise" between team members.

SUGGESTED READINGS

Barner, Robert W., *Team Troubleshooter.* Palo Alto: Davies-Black Publishing. 2000.

Fisher, Kimball, Steven Rayner, William Belgard, and the Belgard-Fisher-Rayner Team. *Tips for Teams: A Ready Reference for Solving Common Team Problems.* New York: McGraw-Hill, Inc. 1995.

Katzenbach, Jon R. and Douglas K.Smith, *The Wisdom of Teams.* New York: HarperCollins. 1993.

Parker, Glenn M., *Cross-Functional Teams.* San Francisco: Jossey-Bass, Inc. 1994.

TRANSLATION TO THE LEADERSHIP ARCHITECT® COMPETENCY LIBRARY

In order for a team or individuals on a team to perform well in this area, these are the competencies that would most likely be in play. Aside from a team improvement plan where everybody works on the same thing, some individual team members may need to work on some of these competencies. A critical number (but not necessarily all) of team members would have to be good at:

MISSION CRITICAL:

☐ 18. Delegation

☐ 27. Informing

☐ 56. Sizing Up People

☐ 60. *Building Effective* Teams

IMPORTANT:

☐ 2. *Dealing with* Ambiguity

☐ 19. Developing Direct Reports

☐ 36. Motivating Others

☐ 42. Peer Relationships

☐ 62. Time Management

NICE TO HAVE:

☐ 37. Negotiating

☐ 45. Personal Learning

☐ 54. Self-Development

☐ 55. Self-Knowledge

In addition to the ten tips listed for this cluster, there are additional tips that may apply from *FYI For Your Improvement*™. Below are the four items from the TEAM ARCHITECT® that make up this cluster. The item number appears to the left of each item. Immediately below the text of each item are competency and tip numbers from *FYI*. The competency is listed first (from 1 to 67), followed by the tip number (1 to 10). For example, 33-4 refers to competency 33 (Listening), tip number 4. The tips are generally written for individual development so some adaptation might be needed in the team context.

16. The team assigns work flexibly to team members.
    18-2,3,5,9; 27-2; 36-10; 37-4; 56-3,5; 110-5

34. Team members pitch in and share the load.
    36-3; 60-1,3,5,6,7,8; 62-2; 65-2; 110-4

52. Team members have the autonomy needed to do their work.
    18-1,2,3,8,9; 27-2,3; 35-1,7; 36-1

70. The team uses cross training so team members can fill in for one another.
    5-7; 19-1,2,3,4,6,8; 31-5; 46-9; 56-3

17

TASK SKILLS—The effort necessary to get the job done

Measurement—Did the team have adequate process and outcome measures to guide its work?

UNSKILLED

☐ Team does not have a process in place to measure its performance

☐ Team does not have well-defined outcome measures

☐ Team does not have well-defined process measures

☐ Team members do not give one another feedback regarding their performance

☐ Team does not debrief successes and failures as a group

☐ Measures may leave out the customer

☐ Measures are secretive and only known by the leader or select members

☐ Team is too busy to take the time to develop measures

☐ Team is too busy to review performance against measures

☐ Team members may be unclear about who is responsible for what

☐ Team has measures but they don't measure the right things

☐ Team members are distrustful of measures; they fear they might be used to assign blame

☐ Team has measures but they are cumbersome and too complex

SKILLED (TEAM ARCHITECT® ITEMS WITH NUMBERS)

☐ (17) The team regularly tracks measures of its performance

☐ (35) Performance improvement feedback to one another is common on this team

☐ (53) Success measurements are open and known to all on the team

☐ (71) This team is effective at creating process measures to keep itself on track and get early warning

☐ Team measures are aligned with vision and strategy

☐ The team clearly creates measures for key processes, tasks and outcomes

☐ Measures are robust and measure both internally and externally, including the customer

☐ All team members can explain the measurement system to a visitor

☐ The team believes that measurement is positive and constructive, not punitive

☐ Measurements are used to improve performance, not assign blame

OVERUSED (TOO MUCH OF A GOOD THING)

☐ Team spends too much time on measurement at the expense of productivity

☐ Measurement becomes a goal and a pursuit of its own

☐ Team members are too direct with each other; feedback is harmful

☐ Team is too aggressive in its pursuit of measures

☐ Team misses the soft or "people stuff" because it is so focused on numbers

☐ Team members are always looking over one another's shoulders and inspecting each other's work

☐ Measuring every breath the team takes can be numbing and intimidating

☐ Team may overvalue process measurement in place of outcomes

☐ It's hard for new team members to get up-to-speed in a measurement rich environment

Note on overused strengths: Strengths used too much or too singly tend to have the negative effects listed above. To decrease those negative consequences, you have two alternatives. You can scale down or use the strength less or you can compensate for it with another skill or behavior. In practice, it is very difficult to get an individual or a team to use a strength less. Therefore, the best path is to develop compensators. Below are listed other TEAM ARCHITECT® clusters that would compensate for overusing this dimension and compensating skills from the LEADERSHIP ARCHITECT® library of 67 competencies.

COMPENSATING TEAM CLUSTERS: 1, 2, 18, 20

COMPENSATING COMPETENCIES: 36, 50, 53, 60

SOME CAUSES OF POOR PERFORMANCE

- [ ] Team members may be disorganized
- [ ] Team members may be inexperienced
- [ ] Team members may not manage time well
- [ ] Team members avoid conflict associated with giving feedback on performance goals
- [ ] Team leader may not hold members accountable
- [ ] Team leader may not be held accountable for team results
- [ ] Team leader may let missed performance goals slip too often
- [ ] Organization has a weak performance culture
- [ ] Senior leaders or sponsors aren't asking for the measures
- [ ] Team members may not be committed to the goals or performance measures

THE MAP

Don't expect what you don't inspect. Measurement helps focus resources on the mission essential tasks. Measurement helps people decide where to put their time and effort. Measurement guides decision making. Measurement lets everyone know where they stand. Measurement visible to everyone levels the playing field. Everyone is equal. Measurement allows a corrective feedback loop to help team members correct their efforts as quickly as possible. Measurement helps direct equitable rewards. Measurement assures that team efforts are aligned with the grander vision and plan. Measurement allows the team to pursue a path of continuous improvement. Measurement makes team discussions and problem solving activities more on point and less on opinion. Measurement creates a culture of accountability. For most, measurement is motivating. Net, the time it takes to design, apply and track tasks and outcomes should pay dividends in more effective and efficient use of team resources.

SOME REMEDIES

☐ **1. Align measures with team priorities.** Assuming the team has set it's priorities along the lines of *Cluster 15, Focusing*, measures need to be deployed against the mission critical tasks, processes and outcomes that align the team's objectives to the bigger picture. An effective measurement system draws a clear line of sight between the business strategies, the customer needs, the team's strategy for accomplishing its portion of the business strategy, and a set of measures that reflects the team's strategy. Connecting these elements gets the team and the business to work together, creates mutual buy-in and support for goals, and ultimately synchronizes performance. So that the measuring doesn't get in the way of performing, it's the mission critical that needs to be measured first. It's the things that really count. If there is energy left for measuring, then the team can move on to the less important tasks and processes.

☐ **2. Use process, task and outcome measures for a complete package.** Outcomes are the easiest to measure. Outcomes are usually very visible products and/or services everyone can see and count and time. Most teams can easily get their attention wrapped around outcomes. Tasks are the next easiest. Processes are the hardest, take the most time, require the most detail, and are the step most teams bypass.

■ The outcome measures quantify the end product or output of processes and tasks performed by the team in terms of products and/or services. They are generally viewed as the primary products or services of the team and are most closely associated with the team's results. The prime judges of outcome measures are the customers. Was it what they wanted and needed or ordered? Was it on time? Was it delivered in a customer friendly way? Did it work? Did it last?

- Tasks (collections of steps in various processes) are the bulk of the work that is associated with meeting customer needs and fulfilling business requirements. They can also be the tasks identified as having the most value and having the most potential for improvement. Teams have to decide which of the tasks are the most important ones to measure; otherwise, the team can get overloaded with measuring the minutia.

- Performance improvement really begins with process measures. The starting point for identifying process measures is to identify those subprocesses linked to the team's primary services or desired team results. What process steps are necessary to produce the outcomes above? These steps can be identified by flowcharting a team's process. There are several flowcharting software packages available. Important to see are the number of steps, how long they take, how much each costs and how much each adds value to producing the outcomes. Real fine-tuning occurs at the process step level.

Whatever combination of process, task and outcome measures a team uses has to be determined on a team-by-team basis. The key for implementation is to put them together into a measurement process that is participative, well supported and monitored for success.

☐ **3. Involve customers in the creation of measures.** Because of their unique perspective, customers will have ideas for team measures that the members cannot readily see. Internal customers provide helpful input as well. Including customers' perspectives gets the team outside of any self-serving framework when it is deciding how it will be held accountable. Asking customers for this kind of input can improve your relationship with them, especially if you follow through on the results by reporting something like, "Our customers said that timely service was important, and here's how we rated in this area, or our average call center hold time is only 30 seconds."

☐ **4. Avoid the most common measurement pitfalls.** Team studies have tracked both successful and unsuccessful measurement systems. Understanding why team measures often fail can help to create value-added perspective when

17

MEASUREMENT

building team measurement systems from scratch. Following are some common measurement pitfalls:

- Measures that are too complex to understand
- Measures that take up too much time
- Measures of things that really don't make much of a difference
- Measurement systems with no consequences
- Measures that are only of interest to managers
- Measures that the team cannot improve upon
- Measurement problem solving meetings where team members do not participate because they have no ownership of the measurement system
- Measures that only measure outcomes, not the path to get there
- Measures that only measure process, not the outcomes
- Measures that chill initiative and creativity

Once the team has created a draft of their measures, do a check against these pitfalls to make sure you won't fall into common measurement traps.

☐ **5. Make sure the measurements are clear so there are no surprises**. Engage team members in the development of team measures. The measurement system needs to model how team members think about doing their collective work. Clarity on measures should be as important as clarity on thrust or the team's goals. If you want people to have ownership for the measures, they need to be able to explain the system to a visitor, customer or business partner. Teams that really understand their measurement system willingly go over their feedback or measurement reports in detail during team meetings. Teams that don't understand measures, skim over measurement data. Even worse, teams with little understanding might have their manager read them the measurement status at team meetings, or do nothing at all. The best way to ensure team members understand is to get them involved.

☐ **6. The measurement system should address the work of the team as a whole as well as each team member.**
If team members can't look at the measurement system and figure out how it directly relates to their work, they won't feel as connected to the measures or as motivated to achieve them. It's important to have both individual and team goals and especially important that they be tied together.

☐ **7. Schedule regular measurement review sessions.**
Measurement should be a prominent topic at regular team meetings. The whole reason for having teams is to improve organizational performance. If a team's charter and measurement system are appropriately aligned, they will talk about measures as if they were running their own business. Consider using a technique where each team member is responsible for monitoring a measure and facilitating discussion of the measure, progress, barriers, etc. at the team meetings. This will help to teach team members to keep an eye on the measurement system and instill accountability. Use the sessions to stimulate problem solving that leads to improved performance. Also use the sessions to make sure the measurements are really adding value to the team and to ensure the method or tool used for measurement is still effective.

☐ **8. Make the goals and measures open and visible.**
Ever notice how athletes keep their eye on the clock and the scoreboard? They're checking their progress against time, the competition and ultimately, winning the game. Use signs or technology to post team goals, data and progress toward accomplishment. It's the idea behind the United Way thermometer. This constant reminder will help to clarify understanding, keep the team involved and motivate performance. People enjoy being measured against a fair and open process.

☐ **9. Hold teams and individuals accountable.**
A measurement system has to have teeth for it to contribute to improving team performance. At the team level, rewards need to be distributed against the measures. Teams that do well need to get a bigger slice of the pie and teams that miss targets need to get less or no pie. The same is true at the individual level.

17

MEASUREMENT

☐ **10. Automate measurement.** Streamlining team measurement systems generally improves ownership of the process by the team. Measurement automation tracks performance data on some type of spreadsheet or database. There are all kinds of tracking software packages you can buy in the market; however, an Excel spreadsheet will generally work just fine. The book *Measuring Team Performance: A Step-by-Step, Customizable Approach for Managers, Facilitators, and Team Leaders,* by Steven D. Jones and Don J. Schilling contains an easy to follow methodology and CD with generic spreadsheets/templates for team performance measurement systems that you can customize to fit the needs of your team. The easier and the timelier the access to measures, the greater impact they can have.

SUGGESTED READINGS

Jones, Steven D. and Don J. Schilling, *Measuring Team Performance: A Step-by-Step, Customizable Approach for Managers, Facilitators, and Team Leaders.* San Francisco: Jossey-Bass, Inc. 2000.

Katzenbach, Jon R. and Douglas K. Smith, *The Wisdom of Teams.* New York: HarperCollins. 1993.

TRANSLATION TO THE LEADERSHIP ARCHITECT® COMPETENCY LIBRARY

In order for a team or individuals on a team to perform well in this area, these are the competencies that would most likely be in play. Aside from a team improvement plan where everybody works on the same thing, some individual team members may need to work on some of these competencies. A critical number (but not necessarily all) of team members would have to be good at:

MISSION CRITICAL:

☐ 35. Managing and Measuring Work
☐ 52. Process Management

IMPORTANT:

☐ 27. Informing

☐ 47. Planning

☐ 50. Priority Setting

☐ 53. *Drive for* Results

NICE TO HAVE:

☐ 13. Confronting Direct Reports

☐ 34. Managerial Courage

☐ 56. Sizing Up People

☐ 60. *Building Effective* Teams

In addition to the ten tips listed for this cluster, there are additional tips that may apply from *FYI For Your Improvement*™. Below are the four items from the TEAM ARCHITECT® that make up this cluster. The item number appears to the left of each item. Immediately below the text of each item are competency and tip numbers from *FYI*. The competency is listed first (from 1 to 67), followed by the tip number (1 to 10). For example, 33-4 refers to competency 33 (Listening), tip number 4. The tips are generally written for individual development so some adaptation might be needed in the team context.

17. The team regularly tracks measures of its performance.

    29-6; 35-1,2,5,6,7; 50-2; 52-3,8; 53-3

35. Performance improvement feedback to one another is common on this team.

    13-2; 19-3; 27-2; 29-1,6; 34-3; 35-7; 56-4,7; 60-8

53. Success measurements are open and known to all on the team.

    27-2; 35-1,2,5,6,7; 50-2,3; 52-5; 56-4

71. This team is effective at creating process measures to keep itself on track and get early warning.

    32-2,3; 35-2,6,7; 52-3,5,8; 53-1,3

18

TASK SKILLS—The effort necessary to get the job done

Delivering the Goods—Did the team get the job done?

UNSKILLED

☐ The team gets easily distracted from its mission critical priorities

☐ Team's poor relationships with others in the organization interfere with getting the cooperation necessary to achieve results

☐ The team is inconsistent in execution

☐ Team talent is not in balance; a few do all the work

☐ The team has trouble making timely decisions

☐ The team doesn't work well as a team

☐ The team wants to do everything itself; it does not ask for help

☐ The team doesn't clarify priorities well

☐ The team is not skilled at designing effective and efficient processes

☐ The team wastes resources going down false paths

☐ The team does not have the necessary talent to accomplish its mission

☐ The team is collectively not very ambitious

SKILLED (TEAM ARCHITECT® ITEMS WITH NUMBERS)

☐ (18) The team is effective in finding the resources it needs to get its work done

☐ (36) Team meetings are effective and accomplish their agenda

☐ (54) The team consistently meets or exceeds its goals

☐ (72) This team is a role model for others on getting things done

177

- [ ] The team is willing to go outside to get help and resources
- [ ] The team comfortably outsources work done better by others
- [ ] There are few bumps in the road or surprises the team has not prepared for ahead of time
- [ ] Everyone on the team works hard and contributes
- [ ] The team always finds a way to get things done despite difficulties
- [ ] The team plans its work and then methodically works its plan

OVERUSED (TOO MUCH OF A GOOD THING)

- [ ] Although the team always wins the prize for performance, it isn't having much fun; the pressure to perform is too great
- [ ] Team asks for help so much that it has exhausted its resources
- [ ] The team's sharp task focus chills creativity and innovation
- [ ] Team meetings are so focused on the agenda that they resist needed detours to raise unexpected problems
- [ ] The team gets unduly upset when something happens with the plan
- [ ] The team is so engaged in its own performance that it doesn't help other teams out when they need it
- [ ] Individual team members resist leaving the team for other opportunities
- [ ] It's hard for a new team member to get up-to-speed fast enough to suit the rest of the team
- [ ] The team is arrogant. Others are tired of hearing about them and their achievements

Note on overused strengths: Strengths used too much or too singly tend to have the negative effects listed above. To decrease those negative consequences, you have two alternatives. You can scale down or use the strength less or you can compensate for it with another skill or behavior. In practice, it is very difficult to get an individual or a team to use a strength less. Therefore, the best path is to develop compensators. Below are listed other TEAM ARCHITECT® clusters that would compensate for overusing this dimension and compensating skills from the LEADERSHIP ARCHITECT® library of 67 competencies.

COMPENSATING TEAM CLUSTERS: 13, 19, 20

COMPENSATORS: 2, 21, 28, 31, 38, 42, 60

SOME CAUSES OF POOR PERFORMANCE

☐ Members may be uncomfortable asking for help; members may see outreach for resources as a sign of weakness

☐ The team has burned bridges in the organization

☐ The team is not ambitious

☐ Team work habits are not strong

☐ There is a lot of noise and tension in the team

☐ Team has trouble making timely decisions

☐ Team isn't comfortable with ambiguity

☐ Team doesn't learn from past performance

☐ The team has trouble making quick adjustments as things change

☐ Team doesn't do a good enough job setting priorities

THE MAP

At the end of the day, it's performance that counts. Consistent performance counts even more. Even marginal teams can get lucky and perform well once in awhile. Strong teams always perform. They get the mission critical products and services produced on time or before, at or under budget. The strong team is greater than the sum of its parts. The team is focused on the mission critical few. The team is balanced. Individual members blend well. There is a well understood and reasonably agreed to plan. Processes work. Adjustments to change and surprises are quick. All hands are engaged. Resources come from wherever. Rewards are fair. Celebrations are common. Customers are happy. When it all works, it is grand.

SOME REMEDIES

☐ **Diagnose the problem.** If you are at this point in this book, there is a team that is not performing up to expectations. There could be all kinds of reasons for the shortfall. Before the team can be helped, you have to get some idea of why. This cluster on getting results could be seen as the result of all the preceding 17 clusters. So one simple way to help the team is to see which of the 17 team behaviors is contributing most to the team's troubling performance. It might be a problem for the team to come up with its own appraisal. Sometimes, people outside the team might have to be asked to contribute information on the cause or causes of the performance breakdown. You can use the following cluster checklist:

- **Cluster 1—Thrust Management**—Did the team set its course early and well?

- **Cluster 2—Thrust Clarity**—Were the goals and objectives of the team clear to everyone on the team?

- **Cluster 3—Thrust Commitment**—Was every team member truly committed to the goals and objectives of the team?

- **Cluster 4—Trust in Truthful Communication**—Was communication inside the team open, honest and complete?

- **Cluster 5—Trust in Actions**—Did individual team members do what they said they were going to do?

- **Cluster 6—Trust Inside the Team**—Did members of the team trust each other?

- **Cluster 7—Talent Acquisition and Enhancement**—Was there sufficient talent on the team to get done what they needed to do?

- **Cluster 8—Talent Allocation/Deployment**—Were the right people assigned to the right tasks?

- **Cluster 9—Resource Management**—Was the team short on resources? Did the team waste resources? Did the team spin its wheels? Did the team go outside for resources or best practices?

- **Cluster 10—Team Learning**—Did the team improve by learning from its successes and failures and the successes and failures of others?

- **Cluster 11—Decision Making**—Did the team have trouble making key decisions in a timely way? Were the decisions the team made the right ones?

- **Cluster 12—Conflict Resolution**—Was there excessive noise and unresolved conflicts that took up time and kept people from working well with one another?

- **Cluster 13—Team Atmosphere**—Was the atmosphere inside the team conducive to everyone performing at their best?

- **Cluster 14—Managing Process**—Were the processes in the team used to do its work efficient and effective?

- **Cluster 15—Focusing**—Did the team have trouble setting and following priorities?

- **Cluster 16—Assignment Flexibility**—Did team members pitch in and help others get their work done?

- **Cluster 17—Measurement**—Did the team have adequate process and outcome measures to guide its work?

There are two additional clusters after Cluster 18 that could also be contributing factors to the team's lack of performance:

- **Cluster 19—Team Support from the Organization**—Did the team get all of the organizational support it needed to perform its job?

- **Cluster 20—Team Leader Fit**—Did the team have the right leader?

SUGGESTED READINGS

Argyris, Chris, *Strategy Change and Defensive Routines*. Boston: Pitman. 1985.

Barner, Robert W., *Team Troubleshooter.* Palo Alto: Davies-Black Publishing. 2000.

Becker, R. and F. Steele, *Workplace by Design: Mapping the High Performance Workscape.* San Francisco: Jossey-Bass, Inc. 1995.

DeBono, Edward, *Six Thinking Hats.* Toronto: Key Porter Books. 1985.

Fisher, Kimball, *Leading Self-Directed Work Teams: A Guide To Developing New Team Leadership Skills.* New York: McGraw-Hill Professional Publishing. 1999.

Fisher, Kimball, Steven Rayner, William Belgard, and the Belgard-Fisher-Rayner Team. *Tips for Teams: A Ready Reference for Solving Team Problems.* New York: McGraw-Hill, Inc. 1995.

Jones, Steven D. and Don J. Schilling, *Measuring Team Performance: A Step-by-Step, Customizable Approach for Managers, Facilitators, and Team Leaders.* San Francisco: Jossey-Bass, Inc. 2000.

Kaplan, Robert S. and David P. Norton, *The Balanced Scorecard.* Boston: Harvard Business School Press. 1996.

Katzenbach, Jon R. and Douglas K. Smith, *The Wisdom of Teams.* New York: HarperCollins. 1993.

Kaye, Beverly and Sharon Jordan-Evans, *Love 'Em or Lose 'Em.* San Francisco: Berrett-Koehler Publishers, Inc. 1999.

Lawler, Edward E. III, *From the Ground Up.* San Francisco: Jossey-Bass, Inc. 1996.

Lipman-Blumen, Jean and Harold J. Leavitt, *Hot Groups— Seeding Them, Feeding Them & Using Them to Ignite Your Organization.* New York: Oxford University Press, Inc. 1999.

Lombardo, Michael M. and Robert W. Eichinger, *The Leadership Machine.* Minneapolis: Lominger Limited, Inc. 2001.

McCall Jr., Morgan W., *High Flyers: Developing The Next Generation of Leaders.* Boston: Harvard Business School Press. 1997.

Parker, Glenn M., *Cross-Functional Teams.* San Francisco: Jossey-Bass, Inc. 1994.

Parker, Glenn, Jerry McAdams, and David Zielinski, *Rewarding Teams: Lessons From the Trenches.* San Francisco: Jossey-Bass, Inc. 2000.

Parker, Glenn M., *Team Players and Teamwork.* San Francisco: Jossey-Bass, Inc. 1990, 1996.

Parker, Glenn M., *The Handbook of Best Practices for Teams, Volume I.* Amherst: HRD Press. Burr Ridge: Irwin Professional Publishing. 1996.

Robbins, Harvey and Michael Finley, *The New Why Teams*

18

Don't Work: What Goes Wrong and How to Make it Right. San Francisco: Berrett Koehler Publishers, Inc. 2000.

Zook, Chris and James Allen, *Profit From the Core: Growth Strategy in an Era of Turbulence.* Boston: Harvard Business School Press. 2001.

TRANSLATION TO THE LEADERSHIP ARCHITECT® COMPETENCY LIBRARY

In order for a team or individuals on a team to perform well in this area, these are the competencies that would most likely be in play. Aside from a team improvement plan where everybody works on the same thing, some individual team members may need to work on some of these competencies. A critical number (but not necessarily all) of team members would have to be good at:

MISSION CRITICAL:

- ☐ 39. Organizing
- ☐ 43. Perseverance
- ☐ 50. Priority Setting
- ☐ 51. Problem Solving
- ☐ 53. *Drive for* Results

IMPORTANT:

- ☐ 1. Action Oriented
- ☐ 35. Managing and Measuring Work
- ☐ 52. Process Management

NICE TO HAVE:

- ☐ 16. *Timely* Decision Making
- ☐ 37. Negotiating
- ☐ 47. Planning
- ☐ 62. Time Management

In addition to the ten tips listed for this cluster, there are additional tips that may apply from *FYI For Your Improvement*™. Below are the four items from the TEAM ARCHITECT® that make up this cluster. The item number appears to the left of each item. Immediately below the text of each item are competency and tip numbers from *FYI*. The competency is listed first (from 1 to 67), followed by the tip number (1 to 10). For example, 33-4 refers to competency 33 (Listening), tip number 4. The tips are generally written for individual development so some adaptation might be needed in the team context.

18. The team is effective in finding the resources it needs to get its work done.

    4-1; 37-1,4; 38-4,10; 39-2; 42-1; 43-1,2,8

36. Team meetings are effective and accomplish their agenda.

    16-3; 27-2,4,6; 35-2; 47-1; 50-2,3; 62-3,10

54. The team consistently meets or exceeds its goals.

    1-1,5; 36-3,10; 43-1,8; 50-2,3; 53-3; 60-1

72. This team is a role model for others on getting things done.
    1-1; 9-1,5; 35-1,2,7; 39-2; 43-1,8,9

19

TEAM SUPPORT FROM THE ORGANIZATION—How well the leadership of the organization enables the team to perform

Team Support from the Organization—Did the leadership of the organization enable the team to perform?

UNSKILLED

- ☐ The organization does not have a clear vision, mission or strategic business proposition for teams to plan against
- ☐ The organization does not have performance measures in place
- ☐ The organization does not utilize a balanced scorecard
- ☐ Organizational politics get in the way of the team having access to needed people, information and resources
- ☐ The organization has not widely communicated the charter of the teams
- ☐ The team may be wasting resources waiting for the organization's leaders to make critical decisions
- ☐ The organization does not respond to requests for resources from the team in a timely manner
- ☐ Leaders of this organization do not reward teams directly
- ☐ Performance measures may be more individual than team aligned
- ☐ The leaders of this organization are poor role models for team leaders to follow; they are mostly individual performers who do not work well within their own top management team
- ☐ The leaders of this organization are not good at staffing teams with balanced and appropriate talent
- ☐ The leaders of this organization are not good at putting the right team leaders in place

SKILLED (TEAM ARCHITECT® ITEMS WITH NUMBERS)

☐ (73) The leadership of the organization sets clear and challenging strategies, goals and measures for teams to rely on and plan against

☐ (74) The leadership of the organization gives the team easy access to the resources, information and training it needs to get the job done

☐ (75) The leadership of the organization gives the team the authority to make decisions or at least get one made immediately

☐ (76) The leadership of the organization uses a reward system that encourages team performance

☐ The leadership of the organization provides the ongoing support needed to keep teams on pace

☐ The leadership of the organization sets team goals that are aligned with the business and cultural capabilities of the organization

☐ The leadership of the organization runs a meritocracy where performance counts, where measured and proportionate rewards are distributed

☐ The leadership of the organization celebrates the achievements of winning teams publicly and loudly

☐ When teams are performing against expectations, the leaders of the organization get out of the way and let them run

☐ The leadership of the organization is skilled at identifying talent and assembling the right teams for the jobs to be done

☐ The leadership of the organization is actively involved in the talent management moves throughout the organization

OVERUSED (TOO MUCH OF A GOOD THING)

☐ The organization overemphasizes teams beyond what the business proposition objectively calls for

☐ The leadership of the organization does too much for teams

☐ The leadership of the organization over-prescribes the goals and measures of the team, leaving little for the team to identify on its own

☐ The leadership of the organization provides too many answers for the team, leaving little for the team to do on its own

☐ The leadership of the organization gives the team so much authority that the business suffers before they are willing to step back in

☐ The leaders are so team-oriented that the organization loses significant individual talent due to the lack of rewards and recognition

☐ The leaders are so team-oriented that the development of key individual talent is inadequate to staff the future

☐ The organization is so team-oriented that individuals do not develop sufficiently to staff the top leadership jobs, leading either to marginal internal fills of key jobs or having to go to the outside for top talent

Note on overused strengths: Strengths used too much or too singly tend to have the negative effects listed above. To decrease those negative consequences, you have two alternatives. You can scale down or use the strength less or you can compensate for it with another skill or behavior. In practice, it is very difficult to get an individual or a team to use a strength less. Therefore, the best path is to develop compensators. Below are listed other TEAM ARCHITECT® clusters that would compensate for overusing this dimension and compensating skills from the LEADERSHIP ARCHITECT® library of 67 competencies.

COMPENSATING TEAM CLUSTERS: 1, 3, 7, 8, 9, 10, 11, 12, 14, 15, 17 (Basically, the team has to do it on its own)

COMPENSATING COMPETENCIES: 5, 36, 56, 58, 60

SOME CAUSES OF POOR PERFORMANCE

☐ Organization leaders are not good at visioning and strategic planning

☐ Organization leaders are not good communicators

☐ Organization leaders are not good delegators

☐ Organization leaders are not good talent managers

☐ Organization leaders hesitate to make tough calls on performance

☐ Organization leaders are not good at measuring progress or outcomes

☐ Organization leaders are not timely decision makers

☐ Organization leaders are not good conflict managers

☐ Organization leaders do not invest enough time in the development of talent

☐ Organization leaders do not understand teams

☐ Organization leaders are not good at motivating others

☐ Organization leaders are not good team players themselves

THE MAP

Without strong support from the organization around it, even great teams might falter and be ineffective. For the most part, this element of team effectiveness is usually outside the direct control of individual teams. Organizations have to create and maintain a comprehensive support system and be team-oriented for teams within the organization to be high-performing. Assuming everything has been done (Clusters 1-18) to form high-performing teams, organizations have to provide a viable and energizing business proposition along with progress and outcome measurements so teams have something to plan and track against. The leaders of the organization have to manage a reward system that is fair and accurate. They have to make and communicate tough calls on performance, chiding the stragglers and rewarding the winners. Teams have to be given space to perform. Leaders of the organization have to delegate to and resource the teams. They can't micromanage. They have to pay a great deal of attention to the talent management process and system. They have to identify and distribute talent. Most of all, they have to make the tough calls and remove chronic low performers from the organization.

SOME REMEDIES

From the team's viewpoint:

☐ **1. Be aggressive in getting what you need.** Teams need to go and get the support they need from the organization. Teams that wait for the organization to be forthcoming will not consistently succeed. Teams need to determine what they must have from the organization that's mission critical to the team. Hard resources? Soft support? Getting out of the way? An energizing mission? An understandable strategy? Fair measurement? An atmosphere that's positive and conducive to performing? Talent? Listening? Running interference? Authority to act? Information? Just rewards? Just go after what you need. Don't be a complaining team. Do something about it. Figure out who to go to and who should go to make your reasonable requests of the leadership of the organization. If teams are getting stuck because of senior leaders, organizational politics or other broken systems and processes, they need to be able to feed the information up to the people who can do something about it. The environment in the organization needs to be safe for teams to do this with minimum risk. Key leaders need to respect teams who have the courage to speak up. Key leaders need to allow teams to make a presentation to them about their inability to execute their charter. Teams should identify the resources necessary for support (time, money, people, equipment, etc.) so the organization will understand what the team is missing (that is out of their control) for success.

☐ **2. Detect system misalignments and conflicts.** Organizations create systems to operate the company. Sometimes they are all good systems that are not in conflict with one another. Sometimes the systems don't work or are in conflict—one tells you left and the other right. As a result, teams need to assess how the organization's systems can help or harm their overall effectiveness. Here are some questions to explore:

■ Do the organization's systems align with its vision, values and goals of an organization?

■ Do the organization's systems conflict with one another?

If you answer no to number 1 and/or yes to number 2, there is a problem. Consider an impact/control analysis of the systems that are misaligned. They could be systems like recruiting and selection, compensation, performance management, recognition, technology deployment, cross-functional decision making, etc.

Have a coach or facilitator help the team with the following exercise.

- Identify systems that are misaligned for organizational and/or team success.

- Identify the impact of the misaligned system on the performance of the team. Is the impact high, medium or low? (Code each on the flipchart.)

- Identify how much control the team has on the alignment of the system. Is the control great, moderate or little? (Code each on the flipchart.)

- If the team has identified high impact, high control misaligned systems, create immediate strategies to resolve the issues.

- Next move down the lists to identify high impact, moderate control misaligned systems. What part of the control is restricted by the team? Could the team rally the resources or support that it needs to get the system realigned? If so, create strategies to resolve those issues.

- Continue to scan the rest of the flipcharts for system alignments that make sense for the team to tackle. Have the team leader share the high impact/low control issues with the appropriate leaders or team sponsors to raise awareness and perhaps gain support to align organizational systems that may be out of reach of the team.

From the organization's viewpoint:

☐ **3. Set the business proposition.** Recent organizational studies argue that most company growth strategies fail to deliver value. Companies aren't focused enough. They aren't sticking with fundamental basics to explain why they exist. No wonder teams fail in organizations that are disjointed to start with. Chris Zook, author of *Profit From the Core: Growth Strategy in an Era of Turbulence*, identifies three factors that differentiate organizational growth strategies that succeed from those that fail:

1. Reaching full potential in the core business; first sticking to your knitting; fishing where the fish are

2. Expanding into logical adjacent businesses surrounding that core

3. Pre-emptively redefining the core business in response to market turbulence

Imagine working on a team in an organization that really had its act together and knew what it wanted to be and how it was going to get there. It would make the world of teams a much nicer place to be. If organizations start to return to a core business model, we can expect some significant changes in the business world that will require the use of teams to execute highly focused strategies. The organization can increase team success by making sure the key organizational leaders agree with the strategy and understand how turbulence might play out both internally and externally. Teams can help to speed up organizational change if they are aligned with the business strategy and resourced with the talent to get things done. The leaders of the organization have to set the strategy before individuals and teams within the organization can start down the path of being effective.

☐ **4. Create a common mindset and get the message out.** Visions begin at the corporate level, setting the course for the enterprise as a whole. Organizational leaders are responsible for cascading the vision to other levels in the company, divisions, teams, etc., helping them figure out their role in the bigger picture; their piece of the action. The most common vision problem that teams have is out of their control: The team has a focused vision, but the organization doesn't. Teams can't effectively survive and perform if the organization doesn't first have its act together. Visioning and creating a common mindset should be a proactive effort that is part of the way the organization does business in good times and in bad. The greatest effort to create a common mindset, however, generally happens in tough times, when an organization finds out the hard way that it needs to figure out what it really stands for. Having a clearly communicated vision allows employees and team members to measure their values and behaviors against a company standard.

☐ **5. Create a measurement system—both progress and outcome.** Teams need a United Way Thermometer. People and teams perform best when there is a fair and visible measurement system. Not only should such a system monitor progress, it should signal change and be an early warning system. Most measurement systems are too numbers-oriented. The current movement toward using Kaplan and Norton's balanced scorecard seems to be more on target. Leaders of the organization have to create, monitor and follow up on a fair and visible measurement system for teams to truly be high-performing.

☐ **6. Create the best business structure and systems possible.** All teams exist in a structure. Some structures are more conducive to high-performing teams than others. Highly centralized structures chill teams. Decentralized structures enhance teams. Reporting structures can either be enabling or chilling to team performance. How many layers are there? Can a team gain quick access to the very top of the organization? Does the organization have communications systems that enhance rapid exchanges of needs and information? Can the team requisition needed resources with the minimum of noise? Is the bureaucracy kept to a minimum? If the leaders of this organization want or need teams to perform at their best, then every structure and system should be assessed to see how enabling or chilling it is. To remove the chilling influences, delegate to the team and get out of the way. If all the other factors of the high-performing teams model are in place (Chapters 1-17 and 20), then the leaders of the organization need to get out of the way and let the teams operate. The teams have to have the resources and the authority to decide and act. The leaders have to be on call to help from time to time, especially at making timely decisions the teams need to move on with their work.

☐ **7. Be active in the talent management system.** Lack of talent management has gotten organizations into the dwindling bench strength situation. Talent management is now a disciplined process. We now know more than we don't know. The research is consistent. The best practices are known. Organizations that follow the principles are reaping the rewards. It's still tough for organizations to execute talent management well because it takes time, patience and involvement from senior leaders. And there are inherent conflicts to resolve. Organizations that are good at talent management are proactive with recruiting, development and placement of talent. They are on the hunt for talent. They mix things up in the organization and in teams. They don't hire people just like themselves. They know the difference between high performers and high potentials. They hire high performers for the technical jobs. They hire for potential in other key jobs. They give high potentials opportunities to do things that make them stretch early in their careers. They throw them on teams. They especially put them on high-stakes projects. They give them visibility. They let them make mistakes. They give them lots of feedback. They make sure the talent learns from their experiences. Don't hoard talent. Set it free, with some strategy in the process. Good organizations develop successful team players who are put on teams to learn something powerful, to have an impact on the organization, and who then move on to bigger and better things. *More help? See The Leadership Machine, Chapters 19-20.*

☐ **8. Recognize and reward performance.** The leaders of the organization need to connect rewards with desired behaviors. Read *Rewarding Teams: Lessons From the Trenches*, by Parker, McAdams and Zielinski. It is a study of 27 organizations that have created best practice team reward systems. Different systems work for different organizations and different types of teams. Here are some of the key learnings from their studies of reward and recognition plans:

■ Customize the plan.

■ Align plans with business objectives.

■ Send the right message (create many winners/few losers, involve employees in the process, etc.).

■ Use non-cash as well as cash awards—create multiple team reward plans.

- Communicate how the plan works.
- Give people feedback against the plan.
- Budget for the plan.

☐ **9. Reward individuals on teams based on the team's performance.** Surveys of both American and European companies show that organizations struggle with basing compensation for individuals on team performance. They worry that if they reward the team and treat all individuals the same, the laggard performer will get the same payout as the team's superstar performer. Or that the superstar will get the same payout as the average performing team members. While it is easy to understand the worries associated with team-based compensation systems, it is important to know that team dynamics could help to overcome the reward challenges. The "inequity" that results from everyone getting the same payout even though they perform significantly differently can actually have a positive impact on the team's behavior. Teams will confront the laggard contributor and tell them to perform or get out. The superstar performer can be given different kinds of recognition within the team (visibility with senior leaders, the rotating team award, etc.) to acknowledge his or her contributions. Compensation is an organizational system. It needs to be appropriately aligned to support teams. Organizations need to get comfortable with having different types of compensation systems: those that reward business unit results, team results, individual results and sometimes a combination of some or all. In situations where teams are relatively independent with clear goals that are measurable, the simplest way to reward the team is to pay them based on whether they accomplish their team goals or not. Individual reward systems for people on teams can ultimately end up conflicting with team performance. Don't tempt individuals to do the wrong thing in order to get a bigger deposit in their bank account if they can reap more benefits by schmoozing with the team leader or drawing attention to their own performance at the expense of the group. For more information, read *From the Ground Up* by Edward E. Lawler, III. The book devotes an entire chapter to making reward systems work in organizations.

☐ **10. Leaders have to listen.** Leaders in the organization must be willing to listen to what the team needs and recommends, then do something about it on a timely basis, even if it is to reject the need or recommendation. Teams need a clear statement of what their tasks are and what constraints or limitations exist. Organizations often make the common mistake of not making teams aware of the constraints on the solutions they might propose. As a result, teams will come up with creative (yet impractical) and expensive solutions. Then the team gets frustrated when the organization rejects or won't implement their recommendations. One of the best ways to kill trust in leadership from a team is to lead teams into thinking their opinion about the decision really affects the decision. Teams know when you are jerking them around. Don't ask if you aren't going to consider the input or if you have already made up your mind. If a decision requires a leader use his or her authority without discussion, just say so. Some organizations use teams as a guise for getting employees to commit to a preconceived solution. This generally happens after they make one suggestion after another (that gets rejected) until they finally get to the decision the organization wanted all along. This may work well once, but after that teams won't want to play the game. Therefore, investments in team recommendations need to be as hefty as the recommendation to fund the team's existence to start with.

SUGGESTED READINGS

Fisher, Kimball, Steven Rayner, William Belgard, and the Belgard-Fisher-Rayner Team. *Tips for Teams: A Ready Reference for Solving Common Team Problems.* New York: McGraw-Hill, Inc. 1995.

Kaplan, Robert S. and David P. Norton, *The Balanced Scorecard.* Boston: Harvard Business School Press. 1996.

Katzenbach, Jon R. and Douglas K. Smith, *The Wisdom of Teams.* New York: HarperCollins. 1993.

Lawler, Edward E. III, *From the Ground Up.* San Francisco: Jossey-Bass, Inc. 1996.

Lombardo, Michael M. and Robert W. Eichinger, *The Leadership Machine.* Minneapolis: Lominger Limited, Inc. (2001).

Parker, Glenn, Jerry McAdams, and David Zielinski, *Rewarding Teams: Lessons From the Trenches.* San Francisco: Jossey-Bass, Inc. 2000.

Robbins, Harvey and Michael Finley, *The New Why Teams Don't Work: What Goes Wrong and How to Make it Right.* San Francisco: Berrett-Koehler Publishers, Inc. 2000.

Zook, Chris and James Allen, *Profit From the Core: Growth Strategy in an Era of Turbulence.* Boston: Harvard Business School Press. 2001.

TRANSLATION TO THE LEADERSHIP ARCHITECT® COMPETENCY LIBRARY

In order for an organization's leadership to perform well in this area, these are the competencies that would most likely be in play. Aside from an organization improvement plan where all leaders work on the same thing, some individual leaders may need to work on some of these competencies. A critical number (but not necessarily all) of organization leaders would have to be good at:

MISSION CRITICAL:

- ☐ 18. Delegation Skills
- ☐ 20. Directing Others
- ☐ 27. Informing
- ☐ 35. Managing and Measuring Work
- ☐ 65. *Managing* Vision and Purpose

IMPORTANT:

- ☐ 47. Planning
- ☐ 50. Priority Setting
- ☐ 52. Process Management
- ☐ 60. *Building Effective* Teams

NICE TO HAVE:

- ☐ 36. Motivating Others
- ☐ 38. Organizational Agility
- ☐ 53. *Drive for* Results
- ☐ 56. Sizing Up People
- ☐ 58. Strategic Agility

In addition to the ten tips listed for this cluster, there are additional tips that may apply from *FYI For Your Improvement*™. Below are the four items from the TEAM ARCHITECT® that make up this cluster. The item number appears to the left of each item. Immediately below the text of each item are competency and tip numbers from *FYI*. The competency is listed first (from 1 to 67), followed by the tip number (1 to 10). For example, 33-4 refers to competency 33 (Listening), tip number 4. The tips are generally written for individual development so some adaptation might be needed in the team context.

73. The leadership of the organization sets clear and challenging strategies, goals and measures for teams to rely on and plan against.

    27-2,7; 35-1,6,7; 50-3; 58-2,8; 63-3; 65-1,2

74. The leadership of the organization gives the team easy access to the resources, information and training it needs to get the job done.

    18-2,3; 27-2,7; 38-4,10; 39-2; 50-2,3; 63-6

75. The leadership of the organization gives the team the authority to make decisions or at least get one made immediately.

    1-2; 18-2,4,8,9; 27-1,5; 35-1,2; 110-1

76. The leadership of the organization uses a reward system that encourages team performance.

    35-1,2,3,6; 110-1,4,6,7,8,9

20

TEAM LEADER FIT—How well matched the team leader is with the needs of the team

Team Leader Fit—Did the team have the right leader?

UNSKILLED

☐ The team leader is lacking key skills for the mission of the team

☐ The team leader does not motivate the team to exceed

☐ The team leader's style is not aligned with the team and/or the organization

☐ The team leader does not align the work of the team to the vision and strategy of the organization

☐ The team leader does not empower individuals or the team to make decisions or perform

☐ The team leader does not provide feedback to the team or individual members

☐ The team leader does not coach well

☐ The team leader does not align rewards and/or consequences for performance

☐ The team leader does not make sound staffing decisions

☐ The team leader does not integrate new team members quickly enough

☐ The team leader does not effectively run interference for the team in the rest of the organization

☐ The team leader is not well connected to others in the organization, including key sponsors

☐ The team leader doesn't listen and doesn't communicate much

☐ The team leader's values do not mesh well with those of the team

199

SKILLED (TEAM ARCHITECT® ITEMS WITH NUMBERS)

☐ (77) The leader of the team has the necessary skills, perspectives and style (manages in a team way) to lead the team to excel

☐ (78) The leader of the team has sufficient strategic and tactical planning skills to set clear and challenging direction for and with the team

☐ (79) The leader of the team lets people work on their own, recognizes and rewards good performance, challenges and coaches the team when it needs to perform better and critiques the team when it has performed badly

☐ (80) The leader of the team runs interference outside the team, is politically astute in helping and protecting the team, seeks information and resources not readily available, and gets external buy-in for team initiatives

☐ The leader of the team is a strong communicator

☐ The leader of the team takes the time to listen

☐ The leader of the team is sensitive to the varying needs of each individual on the team

☐ The leader of the team has a strong desire to win

☐ The leader of the team is keenly aware of his or her strengths and weaknesses

☐ The leader of the team is self-confident and self-assured

OVERUSED (TOO MUCH OF A GOOD THING)

☐ The team leader is a one trick pony, good for this team and for this situation but not good in other situations

☐ The team leader is so closely matched with the team's requirements today that the future performance of the team might not be as good as things change

☐ The leader is so well connected outside the team that his or her attention can be easily diverted from matters inside the team

☐ The leader is so good that it stifles development of individuals on the team

☐ The leader/team balance is so fine-tuned that new members of the team have a hard time fitting in and getting up-to-speed

Note on overused strengths: Strengths used too much or too singly tend to have the negative effects listed above. To decrease those negative consequences, you have two alternatives. You can scale down or use the strength less or you can compensate for it with another skill or behavior. In practice, it is very difficult to get an individual or a team to use a strength less. Therefore, the best path is to develop compensators. Below are listed other TEAM ARCHITECT® clusters that would compensate for overusing this dimension and compensating skills from the LEADERSHIP ARCHITECT® library of 67 competencies.

COMPENSATING TEAM CLUSTERS: All chapters may apply. The team will have to perform under little or no constructive leadership.

COMPENSATING COMPETENCIES: 2, 19, 28, 50, 51

SOME CAUSES OF POOR PERFORMANCE

☐ The team leader's skills are not aligned with the mission of the team

☐ The team leader is not self-aware and doesn't know his or her strengths and weaknesses

☐ The team leader is uncomfortable giving up power or authority so he or she doesn't delegate or empower others to perform

☐ The team leader does not trust the team

☐ The team leader has limited experience or perspective

☐ The team leader is politically challenged

☐ The team leader does not have enough of the universal skills of a good manager and leader

☐ The team leader does not adapt well to change

☐ The team leader avoids open conflict

THE MAP

Even the best of teams needs a leader. There has been a civilization-long search for the characteristics of a good leader. People have been looking for the magic bromide, the silver bullet, the ideal profile of a leader. That search has not been successful to date. On the other hand, we know that certain kinds of skills and perspectives work with certain kinds of teams and team tasks. Consensus leadership would not work on the organizational equivalent of the Titanic. Directive leadership generally doesn't work well with highly skilled professionals. Every team and every team task has a slightly different set of requirements for leaders. Some teams that are more toward the self-directed would need light leadership, where new teams in tough situations might need heavy leadership. So it's match and alignment that is the key. Are the skills aligned? Is the style right? Are the perspectives appropriate? Is the experience and background value-adding? Is the extent of hands-on versus remote management right? It's not that anyone could lead somewhere, sometime. It's more what portion of the leader's skill basket does the leader have. There are some universal skills that help leading almost everywhere, like setting priorities and informing. Since things change more than they stay the same, a leader may outlive his or her effectiveness window. Some leaders are more flexible and adaptable than others and can serve either multiple teams or can shift gears with the same team over time. So the team leadership questions are fit and flexibility.

SOME REMEDIES

If the team leader is to be replaced:

☐ **1. Change the team leader.** If the gap between the requirements and performance is too large to address in a meaningful time period with reasonable resources, it may be best to change leaders. If everything has been tried to help the leader improve, you may need to have the team leader removed from the group. Sometimes you can't fix the damage that has been done. If that is the case, the leader may need to be removed.

☐ **2. Debrief the team when the team leader fails and is removed.** When the team leader fails and is taken out of his or her job, some teams celebrate and some grieve. It could be easy to miss the meaning behind the good or bad experience. If the team leader has been removed, bring in a coach or facilitator to hold a debriefing session with the team. Current members may someday become team leaders. If so, you want to make sure this situation doesn't happen to them. Bad bosses can be learned from. In fact, it is a common hardship that ends up becoming a developmental experience. It doesn't feel very developmental at the time; however, weeks, months or years after the experience it may begin to have some real meaning. Have the coach take the team through a series of questions:

- What did the leader do well?
- What didn't the leader do well?
- How could the leader have improved?
- How could we have helped?
- What didn't we do?
- How can we help the new leader be successful?
- What can we learn from this experience?

Use the results of the debriefing to prime the new leader for success without making it an attack on the former leader.

For the team leader not being replaced:

☐ **3. Understand why teams fail.** Many studies have been done on team effectiveness and high-performing teams. For every successful team found, there are many more that actually fail. Effective team leaders should fundamentally know why some teams succeed and why some fail. They should especially understand how their role impacts team success. Glenn M. Parker, author of many books on teams including *Cross-Functional Teams*, has comprised the following somewhat humorous list titled "Top Ten Ways to Ensure Team Failure." Do these items mirror your behaviors? If so, its time for a little redirection.

10. Don't listen to any new idea or recommendation from the team.

9. Don't give teams any additional resources to help solve problems in their area.

8. Treat all problems as signs of failures and treat all failures as a reason to find blame and downgrade team members.

7. Create a system that requires lots of reviews and signatures to get approvals for all changes, purchases and new procedures.

6. Get the security department involved to make it difficult for teams to get information about the business.

5. Assign a manager to keep an eye on teams in your area. Get them to report all their findings back to you.

4. When you reorganize or change policies and procedures, do not involve team members in the decision or give them any advance warning.

3. Cut out all training of team members.

2. Express your criticisms freely and withhold your praise and recognition.

1. Above all, remember you know best. That's why they pay you the big bucks.

Do you do any of these things? If yes, create a personal improvement plan.

☐ **4. Get full feedback.** Feedback doesn't need to come from the top down to be effective. In fact, feedback from different angles is the most effective. After all, would a team leader's boss be the most effective judge of how well the team leader motivates his or her team or how much he or she cares about the team members? No. Team members are in the best position to give the team leader feedback on a number of things. In order for the feedback system to work, much of the trust and talent foundation covered in Chapters 4-8 has to have occurred. If the team wants to be successful, sometimes they have to bring their leader along for the ride. We don't always get to pick our bosses and we don't always like them. However, when teams are thrown into the organizational structure, we become interdependent on members and the leader for success. Good team players help a struggling team leader who is not performing or leading adequately for the team to succeed. The best way to start helping a struggling team leader is to give him or her the direct, timely, objective and specific feedback needed to raise awareness and improve.

If the organization will make an effort to improve the current leader:

☐ **5. Do an analysis of team leader requirements.** Leaders must be deployed in a way that is consistent with the tasks the team is assigned, and the kind of team he or she is assigned to lead. As mentioned above in the Map, there are a load of research-based models that have to do with leadership skills and team leader skills. Start with the following:

- What skills are needed?
- What style would work best?
- What experience history would be the most value-adding?
- What values would best fit?
- What technical or functional skills will be needed?
- What are the mission critical tasks?

The next step would be to summarize and prioritize the competencies that are mission critical to all of the above. Which would be nice to have and which would be least important? If the team leader were to derail, which competency gaps would most likely do him or her in? These could vary by the culture of the organization, charter of the team, make-up of the team, customer demands, etc. You can use the LEADERSHIP ARCHITECT® Competency Sort Cards or the COMPETENCY ARCHITECT® Electronic Job Profiler to create the team leader requirements.

☐ **6. Provide a personal coach/mentor for the team leader.** We've talked a lot about providing a coach or facilitator for the team in previous chapters. Here we're talking about a personal advisor for the leader. One skilled in human and team behavior who can observe, provide nonthreatening feedback, and create a development plan for the leader to be successful. This is generally an external resource. A personal coach should gather feedback on the team leader from team members, peers, boss, customers and others (via 360° or interviewing) and use it to understand how the team leader is perceived. The coach should also do some firsthand observing to test for accuracy and validity of the feedback. This can be done in team meetings, everyday team activities and even social settings. The coach may have the team leader complete some standardized psychological questionnaires to dig deeper. The key is for the coach to be able to present to the leader the most accurate and complete picture possible. After that, the coach will help the leader devise a development plan that is made up primarily (70%) of on-the-job development activities to improve his or her performance. A smaller portion will also include learning from other key people (20%) and finally, perhaps some training or books (10%) to close other gaps that may be lacking. The coach and the leader should meet regularly if there are serious performance/leadership gaps.

☐ **7. Help the team leader get in sync with the team.**
Realize that being the team leader doesn't always assure closeness with the team. Effective team leaders are also many times effective team players themselves. They roll up their sleeves and do work. They fit in with the team and aren't viewed as an outsider. Some team leaders are better at bonding with their teams than others. It can be especially difficult if the team leader is brought into an already existing team. Suggest some formal team building. Bring in a team coach to help the team with its forming process. Create situations where everyone's skills get discovered and where no one has an advantage because of rank, tenure or technical expertise. Arrange for team members to leave their comfort zones and depend on one another. Use exercises where individual performance means nothing if the team's performance doesn't prevail. Make sure the exercises focus on team outcomes, not individual success. Translate the outcomes into performance objectives and expectations for each member and the team leader.

☐ **8. Help the leader form a support and resource network outside the team.** Research indicates that most people learn about 20% of what they know from other people: bosses, mentors, coaches, parents, ministers, etc. If the team leader isn't catching on to the way he or she should be, enlist the help of some other key people for feedback and development. The team leader's boss could help. So could a key team sponsor or business partner who has a vested interest in the success of the team. This relationship may also end up helping the team get the resources it needs when it needs them, which is a primary responsibility of a team leader. One of the team leader's former bosses could be instrumental as a support person as well. They will know the leader from a previous encounter and may be willing to give some feedback and coaching that they withheld in the past. Consider having the HR partner or Executive Development department assign a key mentor who has the skills the team leader is missing. Make sure the team leader and the mentor know what each person is supposed to do and get out of the relationship. Finally, another option would be to send the team leader out on a benchmarking effort to other companies to study effective and ineffective teams and their leaders. Have the team leader report back on what he or she learned.

☐ **9. Provide the team leader with real time on line feedback from both inside and outside the team.** If you sense that the leader is resistant to feedback, you may need to suggest that everyone go through some sort of structured feedback process. This may be perceived as less threatening than isolating the leader only for feedback. Have a coach facilitate a live feedback process for each member and leader. This will increase the awareness of capability within the team, help all direct their own development, and decrease defensive reactions to feedback in the future. This process will work best after the team has been in place for several months so that members have had firsthand experience in observing behaviors within the team.

- Establish ground rules for the feedback process up front to be sensitive and respectful of member's feelings. Then explain the three rules: 1) State things positively, 2) Be behaviorally specific, and 3) Leave the member in an action state (offer specific ways to improve).

- Team member/leader to receive the feedback leaves the room.

207

- Coach/facilitator explains to the team that they will be making four lists in response to these questions:
  1. What does the member/leader do well that you want him or her to continue doing?
  2. What does the member/leader do that you don't like and want him or her to discontinue doing?
  3. What does the member/leader not do, that you would want him or her to begin doing?
  4. What questions do you want the member/leader to answer?

- Facilitator has written these four questions on separate flipchart sheets and arranged them around the room. Facilitator leads the discussion, elicits responses and records them on the flipchart paper.

- The team takes a break while the facilitator goes over the flipchart information individually with the member/leader who was discussed.

- The team reconvenes with the member/leader present and the facilitator. The member/leader comments on and explains him or herself in response to the flipchart information. He or she may ask questions to the team to get more specific feedback. The member/leader thanks the team for participating in the exercise.

- The facilitator provides a written summary of the flipchart information to the member/leader for future development reference.

- The member/leader incorporates this information and suggestions into his or her style and development plan.

- Repeat this process for others.

Another way to do the same process is to give everyone in the room four colors of index cards. Assign a color to:

1. Things you think the team member/leader should keep doing
2. Things you think the team member/leader should stop doing

3. Things you think the team member/leader should start doing

4. Things you think the team member/leader should keep doing but modify a bit

Each member of the team writes four cards—one of each color—for each member of the team. When everyone is finished, the cards are delivered to each member/leader. In a 10-person team, each member would get 40 cards. Have each member review the material and then follow the process outlined above. The end product is a development plan for everyone on the team, including the leader.

☐ **10. Modify the team.** In rare cases, the team leader may be the right one for the job but one or more members of the team are causing the noise. They are directly or indirectly sabotaging the leader's chances of being successful. So before you abandon the leader, think about the composition of the team. Did the team do the leader in? Changing a team member or two would be easier and less noisy than replacing the leader.

SUGGESTED READINGS

Barner, Robert W., *Team Troubleshooter.* Palo Alto: Davies-Black Publishing. 2000.

Katzenbach, Jon R. and Douglas K. Smith, *The Wisdom of Teams.* New York: HarperCollins. 1993.

Lawler, Edward E. III, *From the Ground Up.* San Francisco: Jossey-Bass, Inc. 1996.

Parker, Glenn M., *Cross-Functional Teams.* San Francisco: Jossey-Bass, Inc. 1994.

TRANSLATION TO THE LEADERSHIP ARCHITECT® COMPETENCY LIBRARY

In order for the leader of a team to perform well, these are the competencies that would most likely be in play. Individual team leaders may need to work on some or all of these competencies to improve his or her performance as a leader.

MISSION CRITICAL:

☐ 18. Delegation

☐ 20. Directing Others

☐ 27. Informing

☐ 35. Managing and Measuring Work

☐ 45. Personal Learning

☐ 60. *Building Effective* Teams

IMPORTANT:

☐ 9. Command Skills

☐ 33. Listening

☐ 56. Sizing Up People

☐ 65. *Managing* Vision and Purpose

NICE TO HAVE:

☐ 8. Comfort Around Higher Management

☐ 12. Conflict Management

☐ 36. Motivating Others

☐ 47. Planning

☐ 50. Priority Setting

In addition to the ten tips listed for this cluster, there are additional tips that may apply from *FYI For Your Improvement*™. Below are the four items from the TEAM ARCHITECT® that make up this cluster. The item number appears to the left of each item. Immediately below the text of each item are competency and tip numbers from *FYI*. The competency is listed first (from 1 to 67), followed by the tip number (1 to 10). For example, 33-4 refers to competency 33 (Listening), tip number 4. The tips are generally written for individual development so some adaptation might be needed in the team context.

77. The leader of this team has the necessary skills, perspectives and style (manages in a team way) to lead this team to excel.

5-6; 9-8; 18-10; 27-1; 32-1; 35-1,2; 56-3; 110-1,4

78. The leader of this team has sufficient strategic and tactical planning skills to set clear and challenging direction for and with the team.

    27-2,3; 35-2,3; 47-1,7; 58-3,4; 65-1,2

79. The leader of this team lets people work on their own, recognizes and rewards good performance, challenges and coaches the team when it needs to perform better and critiques the team when it has performed poorly.

    13-2,5; 18-8; 27-2; 35-7,9; 110-3,5,8,10

80. The leader of this team runs interference outside the team, is politically astute in helping and protecting the team, seeks information and resources not readily available, and gets external buy-in for team initiatives.

    2-5; 8-6; 9-1; 37-1,2; 38-4,10; 42-5; 43-8; 48-2

A

GENERAL PLAN

The following is a general development plan for any competency or behavior that is not directly contained under the 20 dimensions of the team model. This general plan works for individual team member plans or for the entire team in general.

☐ **1. Detail the need.** In order to make sure the individual or team is working on the right things, get more detailed and behavioral feedback on the need. Most of the time, people or teams are weak in some aspect of a competency. It's almost never all aspects of interpersonal skills, for example. It's usually something specific—relationship skills with upper management under the pressure of tough questions from two of the seven on the management committee on topics the team cares deeply about. To find out more about what the need is specifically, go to a few people who might know and who will tell you if you ask. Accept that the team has a need. Don't be defensive or try to rationalize away the need. Say the team is concerned about the need and requests more detailed information so the team can focus on an efficient plan for growth and development. Ask them for specific examples. What? When? Where? With whom? In what settings? Under what conditions? How many times? What signs and signals are they reading? Might anyone they know be of help? Get as specific as you can. Listen, don't rebut. Take notes. Thank them for the input.

☐ **2. Read the "bible" on this need.** Every skill or competency has had one or more books written about it. How to negotiate to win. How to get along with bad bosses. How to win friends. How to be more creative. Go to a business bookstore or go out to the Internet and buy at least two books for each team member covering the need. Have each member scan the first book. Have them just read the first sentence of every paragraph. Don't read to learn. Just read to see the structure of the book. Have a team meeting and

APPENDIX A

debrief the first book. What did members take away from that book? How do people chunk the need? How is it structured? How many aspects of the need are there? Then have everyone read the second book thoroughly. This time to learn. The books may reference or lead to other books or articles on the skill. Have a second team meeting and debrief the second book. Try to answer the following questions: What's the research on the skill? What are the aspects of the skill? What are the 10 *how tos* all the experts would agree to? How is this skill best learned? What are some action steps the team could take to build the skill? Combine these learnings with Step 1 to either confirm or modify the specifics of the need.

☐ **3. Study legendary (either successful or not) teams.** Try to find books or articles about teams that have the skill you are trying to build or didn't have it and stumbled. The Boeing 777 team. The research team that created Nylon. The Iacocca team that created the first minivan. The GE team. The Mars Lander team. *Business Week* and other publications regularly run articles on successful and not so successful teams. Try to see how they wove the skill the team is working on into their fabric of skills. Was there a point when the team wasn't good at this skill? What was the turning point? Add these learnings to the definition of the need.

☐ **4. Learn from a course.** Find the best course the team has access to on the need. It might be offered in your organization or more likely it will be a public program. Find one that is taught by the author of a book or a series of articles on this need. Be sure to give it enough time. It usually takes three to five days to learn about any skill or competency. One- to two-day courses are usually not long enough. You can either send one or a few members who bring back the learning or the entire team can attend. Or you can bring the teacher to the team. Find a course where the team can learn the theory and have a lot of practice with the skill. Find one that video tapes if the skill lends itself to the lens. Throw yourself into the course. No phone calls. Don't take any work with you. No sightseeing. Just do the course. Be the best student in the course and learn the most. Seldom will a course alone be sufficient to address a need. A course always has to be combined with the other remedies in this General Development Plan, especially stretching tasks so you can perform against your need under pressure.

☐ **5. Create the plan.** With all of the detailed data created in Steps 1-4, it's time to put together a plan. There are four kinds of action plans. The team needs to know what to:

■ **Stop doing**—Since the team has a need in this area (the team doesn't do this well), it needs to stop some things that aren't working.

■ **Start doing**—The team needs to start doing some things it either doesn't like doing, hasn't ever done, or doesn't even know about. Even if the team is bad at something, there are things it does in this area that it is probably good at.

■ **Keep doing**—Even in an area of need or a weakness, there are probably things that the team can keep doing with no problem, and

■ **Keep doing but modify**—There are things the team can keep doing but they need slight to moderate modifications to work better.

Ask a number of people who would be willing to help the team work on this skill. Tell them the team has discovered and taken ownership of this need and wants to do something about it. List the specific need the team has decided to work on in Step 1, and ask them for the things the team should stop doing, start doing, keep doing and keep doing but modify.

☐ **6. Learn from others.** Research shows that we learn best from others when we:

■ Pick multiple models, each of which excels at one thing rather than looking for the whole package in one person or one team. Think more broadly than your current setting for models; add some off work models.

■ Take both the student and the teacher role. As a student, study other people and other teams—don't just admire or dislike what they do. One key to learning from others is to reduce what they do or don't do to a set of principles or rules of thumb to integrate into your behavior. As a teacher, it's one of the best ways to learn something because it forces you to think it through and be concise in your explanation.

- Rely on multiple methods of learning—interview people and teams, observe them without speaking with them, study remote models by reading books or watching films, get someone to tutor the team, or use a contrast strategy. Sometimes it's hard to see the effects of your behavior because you are too close to the problem. Pick two people or teams, one who is much better than you are at your need and one who is much worse. Copy what the good model does that leads to good outcomes. Get rid of the behaviors that match what the bad model does.

☐ **7. Get a learning partner.** Sometimes it's easier to build a new skill if you have someone to work with. If you can find someone or some other team working on the same need, you can share learnings and support each other. Take turns teaching each other some to dos—one of the best ways to cement learning. Share books you've found. Courses you've attended. Models you've observed. You can give each other progress feedback. Have them agree to observe and give you feedback against your learning objectives.

☐ **8. Try some stretching tasks, but start small.** Seventy percent of skill development happens on the job. As you talk with others while building this skill, get them to brainstorm tasks and activities you can try. Write down five tasks you will commit to doing, tasks like: Initiate three conversations with team partners, make peace with someone you've had problems with, write a business plan for your team, negotiate a purchase, make a speech, find something to fix. You can try tasks off the job as well: Teach someone to read, be a volunteer, join a study group, take up a new hobby—whatever will help you practice your need in a fairly low-risk way. After each task, write down the +s and –s of your performance and note things you will try to do better or differently next time.

☐ **9. Track progress**. The team is going to need some extra motivation to get through this. The team needs to be able to reward itself for progress it's made. Others may not notice the subtle changes for a while. Set progress goals and benchmarks against them. Keep a log. Make a chart. Celebrate incremental progress. Make sure all team members have access to the progress information.

☐ **10. Get periodic progress feedback.** You can get feedback from three kinds of sources. The team can self-assess progress. This probably would be the least accurate. You can ask the same set of people who helped the team detail the need in the first place. That's a good strategy but remember that they will have a blended view—the team as it was before and the team now. Sometimes it's hard for someone who observed the need at its worst to be convinced much progress has been made. Best is to ask a group of people who haven't known the team before or for long. They don't have a history of seeing the team not doing well in this skill over a long period of time. Their feedback would be the most useful.

SECTION1—TEAM BEFORE AND AFTER PICTURE
Look to the Unskilled Definitions (from—We are more like this now) and the Skilled Definitions (to—We would like to be more like this in the future).

1. From: _____
   _____
   _____

   To: _____
   _____
   _____

2. From: _____
   _____
   _____

   To: _____
   _____
   _____

3. From: _____
   _____
   _____

   To: _____
   _____
   _____

4. From: _____
   _____
   _____

   To: _____
   _____
   _____

5. From: _____
   _____
   _____

   To: _____
   _____
   _____

SECTION 1—TEAM BEFORE AND AFTER PICTURE

Look to the Unskilled Definitions (from—We are more like this now) and the Skilled Definitions (to—We would like to be more like this in the future).

1. From: _____
   _____
   _____

   To: _____
   _____
   _____

2. From: _____
   _____
   _____

   To: _____
   _____
   _____

3. From: _____
   _____
   _____

   To: _____
   _____
   _____

4. From: _____
   _____
   _____

   To: _____
   _____
   _____

5. From: _____
   _____
   _____

   To: _____
   _____
   _____

APPENDIX A

SECTION 1—TEAM BEFORE AND AFTER PICTURE

Look to the Unskilled Definitions (from—We are more like this now) and the Skilled Definitions (to—We would like to be more like this in the future).

6. From: _____
_____
_____

    To: _____
_____
_____

7. From: _____
_____
_____

    To: _____
_____
_____

8. From: _____
_____
_____

    To: _____
_____
_____

9. From: _____
_____
_____

    To: _____
_____
_____

10. From: _____
_____
_____

    To: _____
_____
_____

SECTION 1—TEAM BEFORE AND AFTER PICTURE

Look to the Unskilled Definitions (from—We are more like this now) and the Skilled Definitions (to—We would like to be more like this in the future).

6. From: _____
   _____
   _____

   To: _____
   _____
   _____

7. From: _____
   _____
   _____

   To: _____
   _____
   _____

8. From: _____
   _____
   _____

   To: _____
   _____
   _____

9. From: _____
   _____
   _____

   To: _____
   _____
   _____

10. From: _____
    _____
    _____

    To: _____
    _____
    _____

SECTION 2—SOME CAUSES FOR THE TEAM
(Why are we like this? Why do we do things this way?) Look to "Some Causes" for clues.

1. _____

Comments: _____

_____

_____

_____

2. _____

Comments: _____

_____

_____

_____

3. _____

Comments: _____

_____

_____

_____

4. _____

Comments: _____

_____

_____

_____

5. _____

Comments: _____

_____

_____

_____

SECTION 2—SOME CAUSES FOR THE TEAM

(Why are we like this? Why do we do things this way?) Look to "Some Causes" for clues.

1. _____

Comments: _____

_____

_____

_____

2. _____

Comments: _____

_____

_____

_____

3. _____

Comments: _____

_____

_____

_____

4. _____

Comments: _____

_____

_____

_____

5. _____

Comments: _____

_____

_____

_____

SECTION 3—LEARNINGS FROM "THE MAP" FOR THE TEAM

1. _____

2. _____

3. _____

4. _____

5. _____

6. _____

7. _____

8. _____

9. _____

10. _____

SECTION 3—LEARNINGS FROM "THE MAP" FOR THE TEAM

1. _____

2. _____

3. _____

4. _____

5. _____

6. _____

7. _____

8. _____

9. _____

10. _____

APPENDIX A

SECTION 4—TEAM DEVELOPMENT REMEDIES AND ACTION PLANS

Cluster: _____

Unskilled: _____

_____

Tip # _____ _____

_____

_____

Plan: _____

_____

_____

_____

Unskilled: _____

_____

Tip # _____ _____

_____

_____

Plan: _____

_____

_____

_____

_____

Unskilled: _____

_____

Tip # _____ _____

_____

_____

Plan: _____

_____

_____

_____

_____

_____

APPENDIX

A

SECTION 4—TEAM DEVELOPMENT REMEDIES AND ACTION PLANS

Cluster: _____

Unskilled: _____

_____

Tip # _____ _____

_____

_____

Plan: _____

_____

_____

_____

Unskilled: _____

_____

Tip # _____ _____

_____

_____

Plan: _____

_____

_____

_____

_____

Unskilled: _____

_____

Tip # _____ _____

_____

_____

Plan: _____

_____

_____

_____

_____

_____

SECTION 4—TEAM DEVELOPMENT TIPS AND
ACTION PLANS continued

Cluster: _____

Unskilled: _____
_____

Tip # _____ _____
_____
_____

Plan: _____
_____
_____
_____

Unskilled: _____

Tip # _____ _____
_____
_____

Plan: _____
_____
_____
_____

Unskilled: _____

Tip # _____ _____
_____
_____

Plan: _____
_____
_____
_____
_____
_____

SECTION 4—TEAM DEVELOPMENT TIPS AND ACTION PLANS *continued*

Cluster: _____

Unskilled: _____

_____

Tip # _____ _____

_____

_____

Plan: _____

_____

_____

_____

Unskilled: _____

_____

Tip # _____ _____

_____

_____

Plan: _____

_____

_____

_____

_____

Unskilled: _____

_____

Tip # _____ _____

_____

_____

Plan: _____

_____

_____

_____

_____

_____

_____

SECTION 4—TEAM DEVELOPMENT TIPS AND
ACTION PLANS continued

Cluster: _____

Unskilled: _____

_____

Tip # _____ _____

_____

_____

Plan: _____

_____

_____

_____

Unskilled: _____

_____

Tip # _____ _____

_____

_____

Plan: _____

_____

_____

_____

Unskilled: _____

_____

Tip # _____ _____

_____

_____

Plan: _____

_____

_____

_____

_____

_____

SECTION 4—TEAM DEVELOPMENT TIPS AND
ACTION PLANS continued

Cluster: _____

Unskilled: _____
_____

Tip # _____ _____
_____
_____

Plan: _____
_____
_____
_____

Unskilled: _____
_____

Tip # _____ _____
_____

Plan: _____
_____
_____
_____

Unskilled: _____
_____

Tip # _____ _____
_____

Plan: _____
_____
_____
_____
_____
_____

SECTION 4—TEAM DEVELOPMENT TIPS AND ACTION PLANS *continued*

Cluster: _____

Unskilled: _____
_____

Tip # _____ _____
_____
_____
_____

Plan: _____
_____
_____
_____

Unskilled: _____
_____

Tip # _____ _____
_____
_____

Plan: _____
_____
_____
_____

Unskilled: _____
_____

Tip # _____ _____
_____
_____

Plan: _____
_____
_____
_____
_____
_____

*SECTION 4—TEAM DEVELOPMENT TIPS AND
ACTION PLANS continued*

Cluster: _____

Unskilled: _____
_____

Tip # _____ _____
_____
_____

Plan: _____
_____
_____
_____

Unskilled: _____
_____

Tip # _____ _____
_____
_____

Plan: _____
_____
_____
_____

Unskilled: _____
_____

Tip # _____ _____
_____
_____

Plan: _____
_____
_____
_____
_____
_____

SECTION 5—SUGGESTED READINGS

Cluster # _____

Readings: _____

_____

_____

_____

Cluster # _____

Readings: _____

_____

_____

_____

Cluster # _____

Readings: _____

_____

_____

_____

Cluster # _____

Readings: _____

_____

_____

_____

Cluster # _____

Readings: _____

_____

_____

_____

SECTION 5—SUGGESTED READINGS

Cluster # _____

Readings: _____

_____

_____

_____

Cluster # _____

Readings: _____

_____

_____

_____

Cluster # _____

Readings: _____

_____

_____

_____

Cluster # _____

Readings: _____

_____

_____

_____

Cluster # _____

Readings: _____

_____

_____

_____

SECTION 5—SUGGESTED READINGS

Cluster # _____

Readings: _____

_____

_____

_____

_____

Cluster # _____

Readings: _____

_____

_____

_____

_____

Cluster # _____

Readings: _____

_____

_____

_____

_____

Cluster # _____

Readings: _____

_____

_____

_____

_____

Cluster # _____

Readings: _____

_____

_____

_____

_____

B

COMPETENCY SUMMARY—TOP 23 COMPETENCIES

The following is a list of The LEADERSHIP ARCHITECT® Competencies in weighted order. For weighting purposes, a **primary** competency was given a weight of 3, **supporting** a 2, and **helpful** a 1. This list should be a rough approximation of what the competencies of a high-performing work team should be if all clusters are mission critical.

23 HIGHEST RELATED COMPETENCIES FOR THE FIRST 18 CLUSTERS. (Clusters 19 & 20 do not refer to competencies of the team.)

1st **53** *Drive for* **Results**

2. **50 Priority Setting**

3. **51 Problem Solving**

4. **60** *Building Effective* **Teams**

5. **27 Informing**

6. **42 Peer Relationships**

7. **12 Conflict Management**

8. **35 Managing and Measuring Work**

9. **33 Listening**

10. **52 Process Management**

11. **56 Sizing Up People**

12. **57 Standing Alone**

13. **62 Time Management**

14. **36 Motivating Others**

15. **44 Personal Disclosure**

16. **47 Planning**

17. **39 Organizing**

18. **18 Delegation**

19. **34 Managerial Courage**

20. **15 Customer Focus**

21. **2** *Dealing with* **Ambiguity**

22. **5 Business Acumen**

23. **65** *Managing* **Vision and Purpose**

COMPETENCY MAP (NEXT PAGE)

The 20 clusters are horizontal across the top (1-20); the 23 competencies (above) are vertical with the library number of the competency, down the left side of the chart.

APPENDIX

COPYRIGHT © 2001 ROBERT W. EICHINGER AND MICHAEL M. LOMBARDO. ALL RIGHTS RESERVED.

APPENDIX B

CLUSTERS

Competencies in Rank Order	Thrust Management	Thrust Clarity	Thrust Commitment	Trust in Truthful Communication	Trust in Actions	Trust Inside the Team	Talent Acquisition	Talent Allocation/Deployment	Resource Management	Team Learning	Decision Making	Conflict Resolution	Team Atmosphere	Managing Process	Focusing	Assignment Flexibility	Measurement	Delivering the Goods	TOTAL POINTS	Support from the Organization	Team Leader Fit
	1	2	3	4	5	6	7	8	9	10	11	12	13	14	15	16	17	18		19	20
		3		3		1	3	3	2	2		2		2	2	2		23	30	1	
50	3	1	2			2	3		3	2	2	1		1	3		2	3	28	2	
51	2					3	3		3	3	3	2		3				3	25		
60			3	2	3	3		3					3			3	1		21	2	3
27		3			2	2	3					2	2			3	2		19	3	3
42			2	2	3	3		1			1	3	2			2			19		
12	2			3	3	2	1	2			2	3							18		1
35	3	3	3							2					1		3	2	17	3	3
33	1	1		3	3						3	2	2						15		2
52	1	1							3					3			3	2	13	2	
56			1				3	3								3	1		11	1	2
57	3			3	2	1						1							10		
62						2	2		2	2								1	9		
36			2		1	1							3			2			9	1	1
44				3	3			3											9		
47		1							2					1	2		2	1	9	2	1
39						2	1	3										3	9		
18				2		1	2				1					3			9	3	3
34	1			3		1							3				1		9		
15	1	2	1			1										3			8		
2	3								2		1					2			8		
5	2	2														2			6		
65		2	2										1		1				6	3	2
TOTALS	25	16	18	20	23	23	22	17	18	14	14	17	13	10	14	18	17	18		23	21
RANK	1	13	7.5	5	2.5	2.5	4	11	7.5	15	15	11	17	18	15	7.5	11	7.5			

238

APPENDIX B

COMPETENCY MAPPING SUMMARY

The table shows an analysis of the team member competencies the model predicts are needed to be a high-performing team. We have listed 1/3 of our competency library or the top 23 of 67 competencies (see *FYI For Your Improvement*™). The competencies are listed in rank order from the most important (1st—*Drive for* Results) to the 23rd most important (*Managing* Vision and Purpose). A rank of 23rd doesn't mean it isn't important because there are another 44 competencies that we didn't include. Since many teams don't emphasize all the competency clusters, the analysis also lists the results for each of the 20 clusters. (1-18 are characteristics of the team; 19, characteristics of the organization; and 20, characteristics of the team leader.)

An entry of 3 in a cluster column means the competency on the left is mission critical. It would be hard to be a top-performing team in this cluster unless the team members were collectively good at this competency. An entry of 2 means it is important. An entry of 1 means it is useful in support.

Since the weights range from a high of 30 to a low of 6, you might say very roughly that *Drive for* Results at 30 points is five times as important for success as Business Acumen at 6 points.

Looked at backwards, if a team were not doing well in a cluster, you would first look to the 3s as the source of the problem. If the 3s don't account for the whole shortcoming, you would next look to the 2s. Then the 1s. You would then construct a development plan based upon the competencies the team members were missing using this 3, 2, 1 priority.

The 18 clusters are also ranked at the bottom of the table. That rank is based upon how many weight points were entered vertically for that cluster, yielding a rough order of how difficult they are to perform in general. In that sense, Thrust Management (column 1) is first. Managing Process (column 14) on a day-to-day basis is last.

See pages ii-iii for Cluster definitions.

For more information about the LEADERSHIP ARCHITECT® Suite of Integrated Tools, visit the Lominger Limited, Inc. World Wide Web site at http://www.lominger.com. Contact the person in your company in charge of these products, or contact the Lominger Business Office at (952) 345-3610 phone, (952) 345-3601 FAX or business_office@lominger.com Email.